The Part-Time Adventurer

COLBY FARROW

CONTENTS

Prologue   Pg 1

1   The Call to Wander   Pg 5

2   Learning the Basics   Pg 17

3   Introduction to Backpacking   Pg 30

4   The Swamp   Pg 45

5   The Harsh Environment   Pg 69

6   The Inhospitable West   Pg 92

7   The Red Planet   Pg 133

8   The Subway   Pg 147

9   Thin Air   Pg 163

10   Wilderness Culture   Pg 171

Epilogue   Pg 184

Appendix   Pg 187

About the Author   Pg 191

PROLOGUE

When I think about my job or a new job opportunity, I remind myself of one question: *Why do I work?* I am not asking what my goals in life are or my career aspirations, but rather: *Why do I need to work?* I have found most people answer this question with a simple statement: "To make money"; yes, money provides the freedom to buy things, live comfortably, and do desirable activities, but what is it specifically that you desire to do or purchase?

My answer: to travel places that allow me to challenge myself in outdoor adventure, view natural wonders, and explore new areas. I have been fortunate to have close friends and family who share the same passion for the outdoors. We are by no means experts, but I would not call us novices either; I would put us in the category of outdoor enthusiast. Of the skills and knowledge needed to explore the outdoors, our strongest is common sense.

In my opinion, common sense is the most important survival skill to have. Many people are injured or killed because of their lack of common sense, such as trying to capture a photo inches from the edge of a cliff, climbing a waterfall in a clearly marked 'no entry' area, or not packing water on a strenuous hike. With advances in outdoor gear and the information readily available on the internet, a trip into the wilderness is much easier and comfortable today than it was ten to fifteen years ago. Many wilderness trips can be safely conducted without possessing formal outdoor or survival skills training, provided that adequate planning, research, and gear is acquired prior to a trip.

Before I embarked on what I would consider my first overnight wilderness trip, I had developed a lot of outdoor experience - I hiked in the Appalachian and Rocky Mountains; camped in numerous campgrounds; competed in many mountain bike events; SCUBA dived off the North Carolina coast; hunted deer, ducks, turkey, and squirrel; kayaked in marshes, rivers, and swamps; and generally spent most my free time in the outdoors. I have also been fortunate to have had some formal outdoor education in college and formal SCUBA certification courses. In certain outdoor activities, such as SCUBA, pursuing formal certification is necessary to ensure your safety – you cannot learn SCUBA based on common sense alone. Through these firsthand experiences I learned many common-sense outdoor skills and have visited many amazing, picturesque, and secluded locations.

There are some people who prefer I not share some of the locations I have been to out of fear of increasing the popularity of those areas. I disagree with them and believe that nature belongs to everyone and that everyone should have the opportunity to enjoy the same sights and adventures, as the greater good of the community is impacted by everyone's happiness. To understand this impact, you have to look at how leisure, recreation, and happiness intertwine.

Leisure is often referred to as a state of mind. When a person's state of mind experiences things such as the feeling of being free, getting pleasure while playing, and being able to express oneself freely, one may describe the experience as leisure.

Recreation is typically a voluntary or social activity that occurs within a person's free time. When you combine the experience of leisure during recreation, you can get a sense of why outdoor activities and adventure can create happiness.

Many people are happy because of spending time hiking, camping, and disconnecting from internet connected devices. This happiness can translate throughout the community as a whole because people are able to share the experience with each other. People are drawn to each other when they sense someone is happy because of an activity that is being pursued. If someone sees another receiving fulfillment out of an activity, the natural reaction is to want the same fulfillment.

The common good of the community as a whole is positively affected when people across the community share in the same leisure and recreation activities. This interaction builds a strong bond between people and can expand across socioeconomic groups and people of different backgrounds, allowing them to see each other on the same level.

The ability to share experiences with everyone in the community is simple using social media. When someone sees an intriguing activity at a picturesque destination on social media, it may inspire them to pursue the same or similar experience. Regardless of the many opinions about sharing the detailed locations of certain destinations on social media, the simple act of sharing the photos is enough to inspire others to partake in outdoor leisure and recreation.

I hope through reading this book, someone who has not yet but would like to hike, backpack, and explore the wilderness will make the leap and partake in their desired adventures. I also hope those who have previous outdoor experience are able to relate to and learn from the mistakes and successes described.

I will share many of the lessons I learned while camping, backpacking, and hiking. I will also describe many hiking trails, backpacking sites, and other useful trip planning information for many areas across Colorado and Utah, as well as some Eastern US locations. Some of these trips took place many years ago and I'm sure many of the trails and locations mentioned have changed, so this book is not meant to serve as the primary resource for planning any specific trip described herein.

1 - THE CALL TO WANDER

SOLITUDE

My early experience with the outdoors largely consisted of the familiar environment I call home: Georgia. I could be found playing outside in the woods almost every day when I was a kid. My friends and I constructed bike trails through the neighborhood woods, played in creeks catching crawfish and salamanders, and built forts for camping in our backyards. This constant time in the outdoors instilled a familiarity with the Georgia environment and how to deal with many common elements such as extreme summer heat, humidity, bugs, sticker bushes, and snakes to name a few.

In addition to exploring the neighborhood woods, family camping trips were commonplace throughout my younger years, with areas such as Pisgah National Forest and Devils Fork State Park as frequent destinations. We'd hike mountain trails to view waterfalls and overlooks, and my brother and I always searched for the steepest hills to attempt to climb.

I enjoyed every moment in the wilderness when I was young, but I wouldn't experience the backcountry seclusion that I've come to love until I was a teenager.

At the age of thirteen, I had my first true wilderness experience as a result of my interest in hunting. With many friends and family members who hunted, I asked some of them to introduce me to the sport. Not soon after, I was invited on a duck hunting trip to the Cape Fear River basin.

Our plan was to drive a small Jon boat a few miles up a tributary where we would set up camp and then hunt early the next morning. I was with my uncle, Mike, who made sure we had all the necessary supplies; he had our food, camping gear, hunting equipment, and everything else we would need, including rain gear since light rain showers were in the forecast.

As soon as we secured the boat to the creek bank after an hour-long boat ride, and next to a very small clearing that served as our camp, it began to rain. I donned my rain gear while Mike searched for his, though he quickly realized he didn't pack it. Calling up a friend, Mike arranged to meet him at a bridge a few miles upstream, and then took the boat up the creek to retrieve his gear, all while leaving me alone at camp.

For the first time in my life I was left alone in the wilderness. It was cold, raining, and sunset was only a couple hours away. I'd been left with all the food, water, and camping gear, so I knew I'd be okay. But the thought of being completely alone, and with the knowledge that there were bears in the area, I was a little nervous.

The woods were eerily quiet, as only the sound of rain falling on the water and through the trees were heard. I was experiencing a feeling different than I ever had before. Besides the nervousness of a bear walking up on me or Mike not returning, I felt free and removed from all the tough things in life. I had no connection to the outside world, and I was suddenly unconcerned about what was happening with any of my friends or what events were happening in the world. I was completely disconnected from it all, unaware and undisturbed. It was the first time I truly experienced solitude in the wilderness.

Mike returned an hour later with his rain gear. We cooked dinner, went to bed, and woke up early the next morning to hunt. While I was unsuccessful in my hunting, missing the two ducks I shot at, I had an unforgettable experience. Being disconnected in the wilderness instilled a new feeling in me, and afterwards all I wanted to do was repeat the feeling. I wanted to be in the wilderness as much as possible to take on new challenges and experience new places. I wanted to keep hunting, keep camping, keep going outside, keep learning outdoor skills, and further explore the backcountry.

COLORADO

My affinity for the American West began the summer prior to my freshman year in high school, not long after my eye-opening duck hunting adventure. I remember my confusion upon arriving at the Denver airport for the first time as the landscape was so flat, but then I noticed far off in the distance the Rocky Mountains appearing over the western horizon. The closer we drove to Denver and then to Boulder, the bigger and taller the mountains appeared.

Witnessing the Rocky Mountains jettison out of the ground so dramatically wasn't what I expected and was unlike anything I'd ever seen before. I was familiar with the Appalachian Mountains, which now resembled rolling hills versus mountains.

Looking up towards the steep and rocky peaks, I had a strong desire to climb to the top. While I didn't have the opportunity to climb these towering mountains on my trip that year, I did complete a few hikes in and around Rocky Mountain National Park.

The landscape was drastically different than the familiar Georgia environment. The trees, brush, soil, wildlife, weather, and even the air was different. I realized a lot of my outdoor knowledge wasn't relevant in this environment: the cold was a factor rather than the heat; the dry air was prevalent versus thick humid air; the thunderstorms contained dry lighting rather than downpours; the oxygen density in the air was a lot less than in Georgia; the soil was mostly thin and rocky at the high elevations and dark and loamy at lower elevations, drastically different than the Georgia red clay; the bears, moose, and mountain lions were of concern versus snakes and wild hogs; cliff walls and drop-offs appeared out of nowhere versus mud bogs and swamps; and four-wheel-drive roads were difficult due to large rocks versus deep mud and sand. I was out of my element, but I was anxious to learn about this stimulating environment.

On my subsequent trip to Colorado, I had the goal to reach the summit of a 14,000-foot peak, commonly known as a 14er. With fifty-eight 14ers throughout Colorado, I had plenty of peaks to choose from, and with the added benefit of local friends living near Boulder who were familiar with some of the peaks, I had my own personal guide for a summit attempt.

I'd been warned about the difficulty in completing high altitude hikes, especially for a lowlander like myself coming from practically sea level. With increasing elevation comes lower barometric pressure, and therefore less dense air, resulting in fewer oxygen molecules per breath. At 14,000 feet, the effective oxygen in each breath is only 12.3%, versus 20.9% at sea level. I was in pretty good physical shape at the time thanks to my consistent weekly mountain biking regimen, but my body was still not accustomed to that amount of oxygen deprivation.

Our trip to Colorado was over a seven-day duration, which provided an opportunity to properly acclimate to the elevation prior to the summit attempt: I slept each night in a house at 8,400 feet, went hiking or mountain biking daily, and drank nothing but water for the five days leading up to the hike.

Quandary Peak, located near Breckenridge, was selected as my first 14er attempt. The peak, being one of the easiest 14ers to summit, was accessible by simply hiking up the mountain without any scrambling, exposure, or climbing required. The trail was relatively short at under seven miles roundtrip, but the steepness of the trail was notably present, climbing over 3,400 feet in the 3.4 miles it took to reach the top.

With an early morning start and feeling great physically, we hiked the first two miles very quickly. But once we reached 13,000 feet, I was out of breath and my legs became noticeably weak due to the high elevation. The last half mile to the summit turned into a very slow walk.

A mental game ensued over the final push to the top. I developed a performance goal to simply walk ten steps, then I could rest for ten seconds. My legs were not hurting or sore, rather they were purely weak from to the lack of oxygen being delivered to the muscle tissue. I had watched TV shows, movies, and read about the effects of high altitude and oxygen deprivation, and now it was happening to me.

My mind and body were confused; looking at the trail, I should have been walking briskly, but I just couldn't move very fast. I continued my ten steps and ten second rest routine for the remainder of the hike to the summit.

Arriving at the 14,265-foot summit was a relief. The 360-degree view of the Rocky Mountains was amazing, and I felt like I was on top of the world; the summit was over twice the height of any mountain in the eastern United States.

Even though it was late July, the weather was still cold and windy, and I had to put on a jacket and gloves to keep warm. After enjoying a good twenty minutes on the summit, we headed back down the trail at three times the pace as our ascent. With every foot of descent, the oxygen level increased, and by the time we were halfway down the mountain I felt like I could turn around and run back to the summit.

***

I traveled back to Colorado the following year with the desire to summit another 14er. Unfortunately, the weather forecast was bleak when I arrived, indicating a chance of dry thunderstorms (storms containing lightning but no rain) each day of the trip.

Lightning is a deadly factor on a 14er, and attempting to climb is ill-advised when there's a high chance of storms. A general rule when hiking during the summer is to reach the summit and begin your descent before noon, as it is less likely for storms to hit in the morning hours. Since trees stop growing around 11,500 feet in Colorado, commonly known as the 'treeline', once a hiker exceeds this elevation, they are now the tallest object on the ground and therefore have an increased chance of being struck by lightning.

A few days into the trip, we noticed the chance of storms had decreased one morning, so we jumped on the opportunity to hike above treeline; however, it was already too late in the day to drive to a 14er and attempt a summit hike. Instead, we choose a nearby peak, South Arapaho Peak, with an elevation of 13,397 feet as our hike for the day.

The hike was very straightforward, though it required some route finding and scrambling towards the peak. I felt great and enjoyed the quick 4.3-mile, 3,500-foot elevation gain hike to the summit. Located on the Continental Divide, the summit offered views of the Front Range, including nearby Longs Peak to the north and the plains of Colorado to the east.

I finally felt like I gained a good amount of knowledge on the Colorado environment. I had become familiar with the dry air, the effects of high altitude, and hiking on the rocky terrain.

I was now more anxious to climb another 14er. I wanted a mountain that would be more challenging than anything I had done, particularly one that would require me to really use my hands to reach the top with a route that had narrow ridges and exposed trail. I wanted something that I could really feel proud of and that would test my skills of hiking in Colorado; something that could be considered 'mountaineering'.

***

Traveling to Colorado the next year, we decided to visit the town of Aspen. The most difficult mountains to climb in Colorado, the Elk Mountains, are in this area. After a lot of research and guidance from our experienced friend, we decided to attempt the nearby summit of Castle Peak.

Smartphones were still many years away, and not a lot

of information was available on the internet, so most of our planning and knowledge of the hike came from a single guidebook.

The summit, located at 14,265 feet, was the exact same elevation as the previous 14er I hiked. The hike was rated as a difficult Class 2 hike, with the potential for easy Class 3 moves. This meant a lot of hiking would contain loose rock, steep scree (a mass of small rocks), and exposure, with the potential for some scrambling (using your hands to aid in climbing up and down rock). The risk rating of the route was rated as 'considerable' for exposure, rock fall, route finding, and commitment. These ratings put the mountain right in the middle of the fifty-eight 14ers regarding difficulty and risk.

To begin the 3.5 mile, 3,100-foot ascent, my friend, my dad, and I started at the four-wheel-drive parking lot located at 11,200 feet and hiked uphill through a headwall full of snow. This was my first-time hiking in snow; the snowfield was steep, and I followed the lead of my friend who created footsteps for me to follow. It didn't take long to get the hang of it, and we were making good time. We quickly reached a basin below the summit and then proceeded to hike up to the Northeast Ridge.

Starting around 13,700 feet is where the mountain began to show its difficulty on the final stretch to the summit. The trail became difficult to follow, narrow, and exposed. We ran into some potential impasses but decided to scramble up through them rather than turning around to locate an alternate route.

I was thoroughly enjoying the hike; I loved having to examine the terrain and decide on the best route, needing to use my hands to climb up sections of rock, and having the ever-present danger of a rock fall or falling off a cliff. And on top of that, the perfect weather conditions afforded us an incredible view of the Rockies.

We were almost to the summit, maybe a hundred or so yards away, when we entered a steep section of scree (on Castle Peak, the scree rocks ranged from the size of a softball to a football). As soon as I stepped out onto the scree, the rocks began sliding down the mountain, providing the sensation that I was sliding down the mountain as well. It was a very uneasy feeling, and suddenly I was nervous for the first time on the hike.

Each step up resulted in sliding back down a few inches. I looked over and saw my friend leaning over and placing his hands on the ground to distribute his weight, which prevented him from sliding as much as I was. I mimicked the technique, and soon after, reached the summit.

Many 14ers were visible from the summit, including Conundrum Peak, Maroon Bells, and Pyramid Peak. I took a few photos and then enjoyed the view for a while, as the wind was surprisingly calm and the temperature wasn't too cold.

While trying to enjoy the moment on the summit, my mind quickly began to focus on the hike back down the scree field. Wishing I had a short rope to hold onto for the descent, I was a little uneasy. But I knew this was the type of challenge I was seeking, so I proceeded back down the mountain while suppressing my fear.

Safely past the scree field, the route finding, and scrambling sections, the remainder of the hike was quick and straightforward. Arriving at the basin above the trailhead, I noticed two hikers at the top of a nearby snowfield. Sitting down with their feet out in front of them and using their ice axes as a brake, they glissaded hundreds of feet down the mountain.

Glissading (sliding down a snowfield on your feet or

buttock) is a quick and reliable method to descend a snowfield, although there are risks involved. Not even halfway into their descent, I saw them lose control of their backpacks. Both packs came to a rest high up on the snowfield while the hikers continued an uncontrolled descent down the mountain. Slowing to a halt in the basin, they looked up and spotted their packs a good 300-400 feet up the mountain, meaning they had to climb back up to retrieve them. After making a mental note of their mistake, we then continued to the car.

Climbing these mountains in Colorado, along with the hikes I did at lower elevations, more than introduced me to the Rocky Mountain environment. I didn't have any opportunities to camp during these trips, but I gained a lot of knowledge for planning and executing day hikes in the safest and most efficient way possible.

Choosing the right footwear for the rocky trails, packing gloves and beanies in the middle of the summer, and getting below treeline by early afternoon were just some of the basic, yet valuable bits of knowledge I obtained. My desire to explore places that were a challenge to get to, to be away from the crowds and off the beaten path, and to just be in the wilderness, continued to increase.

SCUBA

I sought after new ways to satisfy my desire to be outside. I wanted to explore new areas, see new wildlife, and be in new environments, but living in Georgia did not provide me with many options to fulfill this desire without boarding an airplane.

When registering for my first year of college courses, an elective course stood out to me - SCUBA Diving. I could get certified as an Open Water Diver while also earning college credit. If I became certified, I would have the ability to explore the countless lakes, rivers, and springs across the Southeast, as well as the Atlantic Ocean; so I registered for the course.

Dive safety and responding to a dive emergency were the primary goals of the course. Topics included knowing how deep and how long you could stay at certain depths; how to respond to an out-of-air event or severe equipment failure; and how to navigate underwater so you don't resurface too far away from your starting point, anchor, or boat. Even though SCUBA diving takes place underwater, I was able to apply many of these concepts and skills to being on dry land and in the wilderness.

I completed the Advanced Open Water Diver course not long after finishing the Open Water Diver certification, and I immediately began diving off the North Carolina coast with my uncle, Craig. We dived near Frying Pan Shoals to spearfish, dived ancient riverbeds over thirty miles out in the ocean in search of Megalodon sharks' teeth, and dived old wrecks near the coastline.

The challenges of being in a new environment, the new risks involved, the wildlife, and the isolation at the bottom of the ocean were all exciting to me. Besides having a few anxious dives where I encountered sharks while spearfishing, became exhausted while swimming against a strong current, or temporarily lost my location relative to the anchor line, I never had any serious issues while underwater.

***

Each time I experienced something new in the outdoors, or even after repeating an adventure, my desire to wander was enhanced. Experiencing so many different environments, feeling the excitement and adrenaline rush during dangerous situations, having a fulfilled sense of accomplishment after completing an adventure, and finding solitude away from the distractions of everyday life, all pushed me to continue wandering down the path to more adventure.

2 - LEARNING THE BASICS

THE SCOUTS

I was very active in the Boy Scouts during my elementary years. The Scouts taught me a lot about common sense in the wilderness, as well as many skills that quickly became second nature.

Building a fire was one of the critical skills learned. We had competitions based on who could build the longest lasting fire, or whose fire could be the first to burn through a string hung a few feet off the ground. The competitions were designed to teach us about different fire building materials and methods based on the goal of the fire.

Pine trees are abundant in Georgia, along with many oaks and cedars. Each variety burns differently, but most are still good to burn depending on the purpose of the fire. The general rule of thumb is a dense wood, such as oak, will burn hotter and longer than a softwood, such as pine.

I built countless fires using different materials and

techniques, providing me with more practical and first-hand knowledge than I would have obtained by simply reading a book on how different types of wood burn. However, relying on firsthand experience vs researching literature limited my knowledge to just the varieties of wood that grew where I lived.

Wildlife was ever present on excursions with the Scouts. A casual hike during a camping trip taught me how easy it was to unknowingly walk up on a snake. While walking with three other people on an open path, I spotted a large snake no more than ten feet directly in front of my friend, and yelled out "snake!". Freezing in our tracks we cautiously observed the snake, a large five-foot long diamondback rattlesnake. Curled up and looking right at us, he began slowly rattling his tail. With extreme caution and our adrenaline pumping, we slowly stepped back and then took a large berth around the snake.

Another excursion with the Scouts brought me to a small cabin on the banks of a pond. We were told to watch out for scorpions when we arrived, and as soon as we walked into the cabin, we spotted one wandering around. None of the scorpions in Georgia are poisonous, but their sting is still painful, likened to being stung by a wasp.

We slept that night with the fear of being stung, but all survived without incident. The next morning, when another Scout was putting his shoe on, he found a scorpion inside it. Shocked, I carefully inspected my shoes before putting them on, and ever since then, I always check each shoe while in the outdoors.

I also learned about night vision while in the Scouts; not the technology, but rather the human eye. Typically, when walking outside at night, I would use a flashlight.

However, while on a camping trip with the Scouts, we went for an evening hike where we were instructed not to use any light source. The first few minutes we walked slowly as our eyes were not yet adjusted to the dark. But after five minutes, we started moving quicker, and then after fifteen minutes, we were walking at a normal pace as we could see just fine.

We were then instructed to turn on our flashlights for just a minute, and then turn them back off. In doing so, our night vision was gone, and we could no longer see any further than just a few feet.

After waiting a few minutes for our eyes to readjust to the darkness, one of the leaders turned on a red filtered flashlight for just a minute. This time our night vision was still strong after turning off the light; the red light didn't hinder our night vision. This is something that was talked about often in books and on survival shows, but there was no better knowledge than having experienced it firsthand.

NAVIGATION

I purchased one of the very first Garmin handheld GPS models in 1999. The Garmin GPS III was revolutionary in the hiking and navigation world. It was very basic with a black and white screen and a very limited road map. I studied intensely on how to use the GPS, how to mark waypoints, and how to navigate with it.

A few months after purchasing the GPS, I went on a squirrel hunt with my friend and his dad. We were hunting on public land in an area I was not familiar with. My friend and his dad had been hunting this tract of land for years, so I let them take the lead during the hunt; although I still took the time to turn on my GPS and mark our car's location with a waypoint.

Heading into the woods with a squirrel hunting dog, we quickly saw many squirrels. The dog would pick up the scent of a nearby squirrel, and then once spotted, would stand with its front legs on the base of the tree. That's when we would look up the tree, and most of the time, spot a squirrel. After an hour of walking around the woods, looking up and circling many trees, we were ready to make our way back to the car.

My friend's dad was leading the way when he stopped, looked around, and then stated that he was lost. He had no idea which way the car or the road was. The sun typically acted as a guide for navigation, but it was hidden behind an overcast sky the entire day, leaving us guessing which way was north or south.

I pulled out my GPS, turned it on, walked a few steps so it would pick up my direction, and then I pointed the way back to the car. Both my friend and his dad were very skeptical, but they had no better choice than to follow my lead. Their faces were shocked when we arrived back at the car a few moments later.

Technology happened to be smarter than all of us that day, and ever since, I always carry a GPS with me in the woods. In today's world, almost every smartphone has a GPS built-in, but knowing how to use it is crucial. Without a background map on the screen, which could happen if no cell service is available, the ability to navigate can still be done and should be learned. Even if the only thing available is GPS coordinates, navigation can still be done, and if a GPS coded topographical (topo) map is available, finding your exact location is simple.

A topo map, likely coded with a UTM grid, is very powerful if you know your GPS coordinates. Most topo maps have lightly shaded straight lines on the map, creating a grid of many small squares. Each line will have a value associated with it, and if using UTM coordinates, will typically be a three or four-digit number. This number represents the first three or four digits of the UTM coordinate. By using certain GPS apps on a phone, and even without cell service, your UTM coordinates can be obtained and then plotted on the map to determine your exact location.

***

The navigation skills I learned during my SCUBA training were invaluable. I knew how to navigate while on land and how to use technology such as a GPS, but knowing how to navigate underwater required different techniques and knowledge. While underwater, limitations prevent the use of GPS, so the sole reliance on a compass is required for maintaining course. Maps indicating depth and natural features are very limited while diving in open water, as many times the depth will remain the same throughout the entire dive area and natural features are absent.

Visibility complicates navigation underwater as well. Even miles out in the ocean, visibility is sometimes limited to ten feet, making the use of any natural features obsolete as navigational points. The almost always present current tends to push you off course as well, compounding navigational error. While the current can aid with direction finding, its ability to quickly take you off course makes it more of a nuisance than an aid. And lastly, communication with your dive partner is very rudimentary, consisting of hand signals and the use of a small underwater writing slate.

Navigating underwater is like trying to navigate on a flat landscape with no trees, without a map, at night, under a cloudy sky, without a GPS, without voice communication, and with a strong wind that is constantly pushing you off course. By learning the techniques taught in the SCUBA course, I was able to learn the invaluable skills to successfully navigate in these situations.

I honed my compass skills including how to correctly change direction to a specific degree variance, such as a 45-degree or 180-degree turn, and how to combine multiple direction changes to correlate my location with my starting point. This required constant monitoring and memory of how far I traveled in each direction, either by counting each fin stroke or by using a timer. An underwater slate was very helpful to write down each direction and distance traveled, but outside of the training course, I chose to just memorize these movements rather than writing them down.

Translating these skills to overland navigation was simple. Rather than counting fin stokes, I learned the number of steps it took me to cover certain distances by walking around on flat terrain, downhill terrain, and uphill terrain. Therefore, if I was without a GPS, I could still estimate my location by counting my steps and using a compass.

Another valuable skill I learned was how to estimate distances with the naked eye. When looking across a body of water, distances can be very deceiving. There's a technique to judge a distance fairly accurately by simply using your thumb, reasoning skills, and a little math, described in the appendix of this book.

WEATHER

In June 2004, I was SCUBA diving with Craig and two others a few miles off Wrightsville Beach, NC. It was a typical summer day in the South where a slight chance of isolated thunderstorms was present, although it was mostly sunny as we jumped off the boat and into the water.

The dive site was shallow, only fifty-two feet at its maximum depth. While underwater at that depth, I could tell when a cloud was overhead and blocking the sun, as the ambient light would decrease.

The last few minutes of the dive I noticed it had become a lot darker than when we had started, so I knew we had a large cloud over top us. Slowly ascending back to the surface after about thirty-five minutes of diving, I became acutely aware of the weather; it was pouring rain, the seas were rough, and the wind was blowing forcefully. None of this bothered us, as we were already soaking wet, so we casually, yet carefully, broke down our SCUBA gear on the boat.

Only a minute or two later a bolt of lightning struck the water less than a hundred yards off the bow of the boat. It was extremely close and loud, and my demeanor changed quickly. We all agreed it was time to go, and we loaded our gear into our dive bags with a lot more urgency.

Not even a minute had passed when a bright light obscured my entire field of vision, accompanied with an immediate thunderclap. We all dropped to our knees and then looked around at each other to make sure everyone was okay. Seeing that everyone was uninjured, we pulled up the anchor quicker than ever. Craig cranked the boat up (which thankfully wasn't damaged), and we got the heck out of there.

The experience taught me how quickly a storm can brew up in the summer and how unpredictable lightning can be. Ever since, I have been more observant of the weather and am always monitoring the sky for potential storms that may be brewing; and if I can even hear thunder when I'm in the woods, I immediately assess my location and relative safety, making any adjustments as necessary, such as moving away from bodies of water or not standing directly under a tall tree.

THE WOODS

I enjoyed hunting deer while I was in high school and was fortunate to have friends with hunting land nearby. Deer hunting was completely different than the other hunting I had done. Rather than walking around the woods or using game calls to lure in an animal, the typical method to hunt deer is to sit still and quiet in a tree stand.

In choosing the best location to set up a tree stand, a great deal of scouting and knowledge of the land has to be completed. Deer, like most other animals, have routines. They follow game trails, they feed in familiar areas, they need access to water, and they do not like to wander too far from home.

The best locations to hang a tree stand include areas that deer feed. Therefore, we searched for natural food sources for that time of year, which included oak trees with their abundant supply of acorns, and other trees, such as the persimmon tree. Walking through the woods and observing the specific trees and berries was something I had never done before; a tree had always been a tree to me, until I started seeking out specific trees in search of a food source.

After an area was selected based on food sources, we had to determine the proximity of a water source to that location. I remembered in geography lessons that water always moved downhill, therefore we looked around at the slope of the land and walked downhill. I sought out natural landscapes that I never stopped to analyze before, including ditches, no matter how small, that could lead us to a reliable water source.

Areas with heavy foliage and those that resembled a hardwood bottom provided clues as well. Hardwoods grow best in moist soil, which is often found near a water source. Also, in Georgia, tree agriculture is big business, with pine trees being the most popular. Trees in a wetland or bottom area around creeks and streams are not permitted to be harvested. Therefore, pine trees are generally not planted in these areas, leaving a more natural ecosystem around the creeks and streams. Searching for these areas with a lot of hardwoods and without planted pines was a good method for locating a water source.

If we found a food source near a water source, we'd then observe the natural paths, or game trails, that a deer might use. Deer like to bed (sleep) in thick areas with a lot of natural cover, and then travel to the feeding areas and water source. We walked between the food and water sources, and looked for game trails connecting the two. Deer, like humans, prefer the path of least resistance, and once I started looking for game trails, they began to appear everywhere. Now, every time I go into the woods, I always notice the game trails, and when needed, I use them as my own path through the woods.

Walking through the woods and seeking out food sources, water sources, and game trails gave me an entirely new perspective of the woods. This knowledge has been useful during many of my subsequent excursions in the wilderness, such as when looking for water while backpacking. If I ever find myself in a survival situation or become truly lost in the wilderness, these skills will give me more of a fighting chance. Again, while reading about these types of wilderness skills is beneficial, there is no comparison to actually getting out into the woods and learning them firsthand.

DISREGARDING THE RULES

The first time I experienced whitewater was on a rafting trip down the Nantahala River in North Carolina. Prior to boarding our raft, a comprehensive safety briefing was performed. A good portion of the briefing focused on how to react and respond if you or someone else falls into the water. From the aspect of being the person who falls in the water, a very simple set of instructions were given: while floating in the water, lie on your back with your feet downstream and your toes up high, breaking the surface of the water. The reasoning for this technique was that most whitewater drownings occur due to a person becoming wedged underneath a submerged rock, with a person's foot being the most likely body part to become wedged.

Sitting in our six-person raft, we floated down the river. Most of the river was nothing more than Class I fast moving water, with a few Class II rapids. At the end of the trip laid the one and only Class III rapid. The water level was high that day, and the rapid was more difficult than usual. When our raft hit a large wave at the end of the rapid, I flew out of the raft and into the water. Remembering the golden rule during our safety briefing, I floated on my back with my feet in the air for only five to ten seconds before someone grabbed me and pulled me safely back into the raft.

The incident felt like a blur, I did not have time to experience fear or excitement. My body had an immediate rush of adrenaline and my mind focused solely on one thing – do not get trapped under a rock. The conditioned response I developed from that experience and the mental image that was engrained into my memory would theoretically cause me to behave in the same manner, without forethought, if it happened again.

Many years later, while traveling in Alaska, I set out on my second whitewater rafting excursion. We were attempting to raft the Nenana River just outside of Alaska's Denali National Park. The river was completely different than those of the Southeast. Rather than long sections of flat water followed by a short rapid, the Nenana was a constant Class II paddle with numerous sections of Class III and Class IV rapids.

With our trip taking place in late May, the air temperature was still a cool fifty degrees. The river water was a frigid thirty-five degrees as a result of being fed directly from a glacier not too far upstream, and scattered along the banks of the river were thick sheets of ice still present from the winter season. The combination of cold air and water presented a serious threat of hypothermia if someone fell overboard; therefore drysuits were required for everyone.

We were given a safety briefing on the bus ride to the launch site. The guide asked if we had been rafting before, and after everyone said yes, he asked us what to do if someone falls overboard. Everyone, including myself, agreed that the best thing to do was to float on your back with your feet up, facing downstream, and wait for a raft to pick you up.

The guide responded with an astounding "no!". He said to forget everything that was ever taught to us about falling overboard, and that the widely known rule we all knew didn't apply on the Nenana. I had a firsthand, engrained emotional experience with falling out on a

Class III rapid and knew the technique worked, so I was confused with the new set of instructions.

The difference between the Nenana in late May and almost every other river in North America was the frigid water temperature. Even with a drysuit on, the shock of hitting the cold water, along with the ability to quickly become hypothermic, could create a deadly situation if someone fell overboard and simply floated down river waiting for someone on a raft to grab them.

The rapids on the river were also prolonged, with some sections of Class II-III rapids extending for over half a mile, complicating a rescue attempt even further.

Instead of floating on our backs, the guides instructed us to immediately look for a raft and follow the directions of the guide. The guide would point for us to either swim to shore, swim towards another raft, or swim back towards them; the opposite of most rafting instructions and what I had already engrained in my memory.

The rafting trip went off without a hitch, and no one in any raft fell overboard. But I learned that just because something was commonly accepted as the golden rule, and even though all other rafting guides attempt to embed the rule into your memory, sometimes it is not the correct thing to do, so it is always imperative to pay attention to all wilderness safety briefings.

I have read many survival books, but one of my favorites is Laurence Gonzales's book *Deep Survival*. In it he says "The practice of Zen teaches that it is impossible to add anything more to a cup that is already full. If you pour in more tea, it simply spills over and is wasted. The same is true of the mind. A closed attitude, and attitude that says, 'I already know,' may cause you to miss important information."

If I went into the trip with a closed attitude and had

not paid attention to the safety briefing, since I thought I already knew exactly what to do, then the consequences could have been detrimental if I fell overboard.

3 - INTRODUCTION TO BACKPACKING

CAMP FOOD

I enjoyed camping when I was a teenager, going at least four times a year while usually staying in an established campground. In the mountains of North Georgia and Western North Carolina, a slew of National Forest and State Park campgrounds were my favorite places to camp.

Without owning the proper gear or having a knowledge base to go backpacking when I was in high school, I sought after remote campgrounds with little to no facilities, yet were still accessible by car. This type of camping required standard camping supplies, such as a tent and a sleeping bag, and there was little concern of forgetting something, as jumping in the car to drive to a store was always an option.

My first experience camping away from a car, where I had to put extensive thought into what I needed to and didn't need to pack, was part of a college course during my freshman year.

The course consisted of a single backpacking trip. The

trail we were required to hike was four miles round-trip, on very flat terrain, and in a well populated state park. It was scheduled to be a very short trip, lasting less than sixteen hours, and with a group of about twenty people.

Prior to the trip, since I did not own a backpacking backpack, I borrowed an old military rucksack from a friend. I also did not own any specialized backpacking gear, so I proceeded with all my standard camping supplies. The weather forecast indicated pleasant conditions with no chance of rain and low temperatures in the fifties, so rain gear and warm clothing were not essential.

Figuring out a meal for camp was the most difficult aspect of the pre-trip planning, as each person was required to bring and cook their own meals. A freeze-dried dish or MRE would have been the easiest option, but class rules stated our meals had to be cooked. I choose to bring a couple hamburger patties packed in a small, soft-sided cooler, and a camping stove with a griddle to cook on.

My pack was heavy from all the cooking gear, which was unsettling as we were only camping one night. I was in pretty good shape and only had a two-mile hike on flat terrain to reach camp, so I decided to just suck it up and carry the heavy pack.

The hike to camp turned out to be very easy, and since we had a large group, our pace was very slow. A lot of my classmates were out of shape, so we stopped every ten minutes to rest. Arriving at camp an hour and a half later, I set up my tent, helped others set up their tents, and then cooked dinner. The next morning, everyone was packed up and hiking out before 9:00 A.M., and back at the car before 10:30 A.M.

While the burger turned out great, it was a mistake for

me to bring. First, one of the most important rules in backpacking is maintaining a reasonable pack weight; I typically shoot for thirty-five pounds max. With the need to keep the hamburger meat cool, I needed a small cooler with some ice. This added at least four pounds to my pack.

My camp stove was also large, but I needed it to support the griddle. This added three to five more pounds. Lastly, I needed a griddle to cook on, which added another four to five pounds. This one meal required me to carry an additional ten to fifteen pounds of gear. With my current set up today, I can pack food and cooking equipment for a total of three to five pounds.

Even though I was hindered since we were not allowed to use freeze dried meals or MREs, and the meal had to be cooked, I still should have packed something that didn't need to be kept cool, and something that didn't need to be cooked on a griddle. If I were to repeat the trip today, I would have packed pasta, such as ramen noodles; a little water, a small pot, and a small stove is all that's needed to prepare a tasty pasta meal.

CAMPSITE SELECTION

Two years later, in 2006, is when I attempted my first true wilderness backpacking trip. I was in college and going with a friend of mine, Michael. I had been friends with Michael since the first grade, or for about fifteen years. Most of my outdoor experiences around my hometown had been with him, including many camping, kayaking, and hunting excursions. He was so enthusiastic about the outdoors that he chose to major in Leisure Management and Recreation, with aspirations to become a camp counselor.

The hike was on a section of the Appalachian Trail in Georgia, located in the Raven Cliffs Wilderness Area, just outside the town of Helen. I didn't know much about the area and relied on Michael to do all of the planning, as he had been to this location before. He said the hike would be short, a little uphill, and relatively easy.

I did not research the trail or dig into any details about the area, but rather I focused my pre-trip planning on packing the necessary gear. I figured I did not need to spend extra time planning since it was just a one-night trip on a short section of well-used trail, and I trusted Michael and his experience.

I still did not own a lot of gear for this type of camping, as mine was more suited for car camping; my gear was heavy and bulky and not very favorable for backpacking. Luckily, the university I attended had a strong outdoor recreation program which allowed me to rent some gear, most importantly a backpack.

I owned a four-person Kelty tent with a lot of room to spread out and stash gear, however, it was bulky and heavy, weighing about nine or ten pounds. I ultimately decided to bring it on the trip because I did not want to rent a backpacking tent; and I didn't think the few extra pounds would make much of a difference. Plus, the extra room in the tent would be nice.

I had a sleeping pad that was fairly comfortable and lightweight, though it was made of thick foam and was very bulky; I could not even fit it inside my backpack. I ended up having to strap it to the outside of my pack next to my bulky and heavy tent, as the tent would not fit inside my pack either.

Other gear included the typical things I would bring on a camping trip, such as a flashlight, knife, water, camping stove, food, lighter, small pillow, camera, extra clothes, and other small pieces of gear. Needless to say, my pack was very heavy and bulky. I would quickly learn on this trip, along with future trips in the Appalachian Mountains, many lessons on what is necessary to pack, what is nice to pack, and what is overkill.

***

The parking lot at the trailhead was empty when we arrived shortly after lunch on a fall, Saturday afternoon. Initially hiking about one mile uphill with 600 feet of elevation gain, we walked out onto the summit of Cowrock and had an amazing view of the mountains. I was very winded from carrying my heavy and bulky pack, yet I wasn't sweating much since the temperature was so cold; there was even a little sleet and snow still on the ground from a previous storm.

Continuing past Cowrock on a relatively flat trail, we came across an area that looked great for a campsite. It was well sheltered by the trees, but there wasn't a grand view of the mountains like we were searching for. The site was only a quarter mile past Cowrock and we were not ready to quit hiking, so we decided to keep pushing forward to see if we could find a better site.

The trail steepened and climbed another 600 feet over the next mile. We were winded again from our heavy packs and the uphill hiking, so we made the decision to stop at the next clearing and set up camp.

When we reached the top of the mountain, Wolf Laurel Top, we came across a clearing measuring about 30x30 feet. There was a small fire ring built with rocks and one of the most amazing views in Georgia overlooking the Raven Cliffs Wilderness Area.

We immediately agreed this would be our campsite for the night and we quickly set up our tent and made camp.

I pulled out a small chair I had packed, a very heavy and unnecessary chair, but it felt great to sit down and take in the view.

We wanted to build a fire, so we gathered as much wood as we could. Since we were directly on top of the mountain, most of the trees and shrubbery were small in stature, resulting in nothing but small twigs for firewood. Our fire wasn't very big, but a large fire isn't necessary to keep warm; even a small fire will keep two people warm if you stay close to it.

The sunset that time of year was around 6:00 P.M. Shortly before sunset, the wind picked up and the temperature dropped quickly into the lower thirties, with the forecast for the overnight low to be in the mid-twenties. That sort of temperature is usually not an issue, and since we checked the forecast, we were prepared with beanies, gloves, and fleece jackets. The one thing we did not check, and the condition that is amplified while on the top of an exposed mountain, is the wind.

Wind is very common and almost always present on the top of a mountain. We knew it was going to be cold, but we did not account for the exposure of our campsite and the accompanying wind chill.

We tried to keep warm by staying close to the fire, but quickly learned a valuable lesson about being in the wilderness: When a steady fifteen to twenty-five mile per hour wind is present, and a fire is exposed directly to that wind, most of the heat from the fire will be immediately dispersed and lost. We tried to keep our hands directly downwind of the fire but were unable to get any true warmth.

Already chilled from the cold and wind, we cooked dinner a little early in hopes it would warm us up. We packed a small butane stove called a PocketRocket. The stove was designed for backpacking, as it was compact and lightweight, making it a much better option than the heavy stove I used a couple years prior.

The food we packed consisted of Mountain House freeze-dried meals. Preparing the meal was supposed to be simple. We would boil some water, pour the boiling water into the food packet, and then wait about eight to twelve minutes for it to cook.

I read the instructions printed on the side of the packet. It said to add two cups of boiling water to the pouch, then wait ten minutes before eating. I looked at Michael and asked him how I was supposed to measure two cups of water, as I did not pack a measuring cup. He said to use my Nalgene (plastic water bottle).

I picked up the Nalgene and noticed pre-marked measurements on the side of the bottle. I had never noticed the measurements before, but now it was so apparent, and it made perfect sense. The measurements were provided in both ML and OZ, but not cups. Luckily, Michael knew his conversions better than me, and said there were eight ounces in one cup.

The gas was turned on and the stove was lit. We placed a metal pot filled with water on top of the PocketRocket's flame and waited for a boil, which would usually take between one and three minutes depending on the amount of water.

A few minutes went by and the water looked warm, but didn't appear to be near boiling; I even dipped my fingers into the water with no issue. We quickly realized that similar to the heat dispersion with our fire, we had the same issue with our stove; the wind was blowing the heat away from the pot.

Needing to block the wind, we built a windbreak with stacked rocks on the windward side of the stove, put our bodies in a position to block the wind, and then using aluminum foil, we built a heat trap along the leeward side of the stove. The water finally boiled after another three or four minutes.

The resulting meal, which provided excellent hand warmth while it cooked, was one of the best meals I ever had in the wilderness. Since the meal was prepared with boiling water, the food was hot and worked well at warming us up. But as quickly as the warmth filled our bodies while we ate, the chill returned as soon as we finished. It was only 7:00 P.M., the sun had just set, and we were both very cold. Neither one of us were tired, but we decided to get inside our tent and into our sleeping bags just to stay warm.

We wished we had stopped to camp at the clearing near Cowrock, as there would have been less wind, but because of our bad decision to camp on the summit, exposed to the wind on a very cold night, we were unable to enjoy a relaxing evening.

We woke up the next morning before sunrise. The air was chilly, but completely calm. The sun slowly appeared over the mountains and provided us with an amazing sunrise. I asked myself if this made up for the misery last night. We could have camped at the other location, woken up twenty minutes earlier, and hiked to the same summit to enjoy the sunrise.

We ate a quick breakfast consisting of energy bars and hot tea, and then packed our gear and headed back down the mountain to the car.

Michael tending to the fire at camp
***

I learned an important lesson that will always be on my mind while selecting a campsite. Mountain areas generally experience more wind than valleys, with increasing wind speeds the higher up in elevation you are. The effects of the persistent winds can be observed simply by looking at the smaller size and the windblown shape of the trees near a summit. Anytime I see a summit with a view that is vast and unobstructed, I know the wind will have no resistance and will be more intense than in the surrounding areas.

With every camping trip I have planned since this experience, I have looked at more than just the precipitation and temperature forecast, but also the wind. What is the maximum wind speed? What is the resulting wind chill? What is the wind direction? Then, when I find a potential campsite, I take into consideration the natural windbreaks and their relative location to the wind direction.

Even with how miserable we were at times, I still

consider the trip a great success and great memory. The view from the campsite, the amazing sunrise, and the fact that we saw no other person during the trip was awesome.

As soon as I made it back home, the realization of how much I had taken common comforts in life for granted set in, such as having a car nearby, a climate-controlled house with a roof and walls, a hot shower, a stove, a toilet, and a comfortable bed.

The trip also taught me to just go do the things you want to do, rather than wait for the perfect time or when it may be more convenient. People often put off doing things to the next week, the next month, or the next year, rather than just going outside and doing it. Even if the weather may not be perfect, or the upcoming week may look stressful, it does not mean a trip should be postponed.

I am thankful I did not postpone this trip because of some meaningless excuse, such as needing to study for an upcoming quiz. While I hunted a lot with Michael, and car camped many times with him as well, this was the first and only time I completed a backpacking trip with him, as he passed away the following year at the age of 23.

ILLNESS

My next backpacking trip took place a year later. This time I wanted to step it up a notch and complete two nights of camping. My brother, Christopher, was accompanying me on the trip, and similar to me, he had a lot of car camping experience. But even being three years older than me, he had never been backpacking before, and did not have as much wilderness experience as me at the time.

We drove two cars so we could complete a point-to-point hike versus an out-and-back. Parking one car at Tesnatee Gap, which would serve as our exit point, we then drove the other car further south and parked at Woody Gap.

We planned to start our Appalachian Trail hike at Woody Gap, then hike a total of sixteen miles over the next three days to Tesnatee Gap. The first night we initially planned to camp near the Blood Mountain shelter, which was near the summit of Blood Mountain. Then for the second night, we had planned to camp near Cowrock, possibly at the site I had passed up the previous year.

The weather forecast was poor and included rain, temperatures in the forties, and a moderate wind. With this unpleasant forecast and my previous experience with high winds, we modified our first night's plan in order to camp prior to the shelter and at a lower elevation, in an area sheltered by the trees.

Looking at our map, an area called Bird Gap was located immediately before the trail ascended steeply to the summit of Blood Mountain. By agreeing on this site, it would make our first day's hike a very manageable 6.5 miles.

***

The hike started off great. There was a light mist and a moderate wind, but we were not deterred by the weather. The trail had a good mixture of uphill and downhill hiking, yet there were no sustained climbs or any significant elevation gain. A few times we passed by what appeared to be a ledge or overlook, but the fog was so dense we could not see more than a hundred feet out.

After hiking for three to four hours, we arrived at Bird Gap, and knew going any further would put us at risk for high winds higher up on the mountain. The clearing and camping spots at Bird Gap were very apparent and looked good, so we decided to stop and make camp there for the night.

With a similar cooking setup as my previous trip, I had a freeze-dried meal to prepare for dinner. Christopher decided to bring canned food. He opened a large can of beef stew, which looked and smelled great. But knowing it added more weight to his pack than my freeze-dried meal, I was happy with my dinner choice.

That night, I was awoken more than once by the sound of Christopher getting out of the tent; I assumed he drank too much water while hiking earlier and that he needed to pee. Besides feeling a little bad for him, since it was raining and cold, I thought nothing else of it and went back to sleep.

Waking up to my alarm in the morning, Christopher was already wide awake, sitting up in his sleeping bag, appearing unwell. Asking him if everything was okay, he said "no."

He had been up all night with a stomach virus. A stomach virus is miserable anytime, imagine it while in the wilderness, six miles away from the car, in the rain and the cold, and without the proper medications or supplements.

We needed to decide on what to do that day, as obviously he was in no shape to continue as planned. While he tried to rest, I prepared my breakfast and thought of what general options we had.

The two options I came up with were 1) to stay put and camp there for a second night, with the hope that he'd be well enough to hike out the next day, or 2) we could try to hike out that day and drive home.

I knew there was only one thought going through

Christopher's head, and that was to be back in a familiar environment, somewhere that felt safe. In our current situation, this familiar environment was the car, and the familiar way to get to the car was via the trail we came in on. While getting back to the car was my first instinct as well, I knew that assessing a situation fully before following your emotions is critical. So, before I discussed the options with him, I took out my topo map and looked for any alternative routes for getting out, as there is usually more than one option available.

The obvious route back to the car was via the trail we hiked in. We already knew the route, and it was on a moderately trafficked trail, meaning if his condition worsened, it was likely we could get help from another hiker.

When I looked at the map, I searched for nearby trails and roads that may have offered an easier or shorter route, though nothing obvious stood out.

I looked at going farther up the trail and over Blood Mountain to the next road crossing, but it appeared to be a steep trail and would have required us to figure out a way back to the car.

I looked for any nearby Forest Service roads where I could leave him and our gear, hike to the car alone, then drive back to pick him up.

After a thorough review of the map, I decided not to choose any options that would leave him alone, require us to find a ride back to the car, or involve us leaving the main trail. Therefore, I suggested we either wait it out for a day or hike out that day using the trail we hiked in. Christopher chose to go ahead and attempt to hike out.

He was unable to eat any of the food he packed, as it made him nauseous and vomit, but I had recently become aware of a new type of energy food called Sport Beans.

These Sport Beans were very light on the stomach and contained a lot of electrolytes, theoretically a great combination for someone with a stomach virus.

I suggested he eat some, which he reluctantly did. Not long after, he said it had helped a lot with his energy level and overall feeling, and it was not making him nauseous.

Before we started the hike out, and in an effort to reduce pack weight, we transferred a lot of gear from his pack into mine. While unloading Christopher's gear there were many unnecessary and heavy items, including a large battery-operated spotlight that weighed at least five pounds. I asked him why he brought a spotlight backpacking, to which he was already asking himself the same question; a headlamp or handheld flashlight is all that is needed.

I quickly realized that my trip preparation had solely focused on my own gear, making sure it consisted of lightweight, compact, and necessary items, rather than coordinating with Christopher to ensure he did the same. Loading my pack with as much of his gear as I could fit, he was left with around fifteen to twenty pounds of weight to carry, and me with forty-five to fifty pounds. We ended up resting every fifteen minutes on the hike, slowly making it back to the car in about four to five hours.

***

Just like my previous backpacking trips, this trip taught me a lot. It's difficult to control when and where you get sick or become injured, so the best practice prior to any trip in the backcountry is to plan for an unexpected illness or injury.

Planning to be resilient in such an event should be done and should include things such as always having at least one extra meal in case the need arises to stay put for an extra night; to have a method for purifying additional water than what was expected; to always study topo and aerial maps to see where possible entry and exit points may exist along the trail; to bring a small, custom first aid kit, with additional medications and supplies than typically found in your off-the-shelf kit; to always pack Sport Beans, not just for a trail snack, but also for an upset stomach; to put a plan in place with your hiking partner(s) about what to do in the event of a medical emergency, such as who would go for help and who would stay put; to carry a small satellite distress beacon, which when activated, would notify emergency personnel of your exact location and that you are in distress; to leave a proposed itinerary with your emergency contacts, and a plan in place on who they should notify if no contact has been made by a certain day or time.

In addition to preparing for a medical situation in the wilderness, this trip also taught me to check with my hiking partner(s) in advance regarding what gear to bring. I have started creating a shared packing list for each trip. This allows us to share gear knowledge with each other, make sure we do not forget something crucial, and avoid packing redundant or unnecessary gear.

And again, I learned that weight is your enemy while backpacking. Keep it light and you will have a much more enjoyable and comfortable trip.

4 - THE SWAMP

SINKING BOATS

In southern Georgia, nestled against the Florida border, lies the Okefenokee Swamp. The swamp is approximately 700 square miles (438,000 acres) with the majority being a National Wildlife Refuge established in 1937. The extreme remoteness of the swamp and lack of artificial light makes it the only location in Georgia recognized as an International Dark Sky Place.

During the early 1900's, loggers in search of valuable cyprus built canals throughout the swamp in an attempt to drain the wetlands. The loggers were successful in removing thousands of trees but were unable to drain the swamp. As a result of their failed attempt, these canals, along with some natural waterways, now serve as access deep into the swamp for outdoor enthusiasts.

The Okefenokee is made up of rivers, lakes, forests, and prairies. A lot of these forests and prairies appear to be stable dry land, yet the forest floor and peat moss are simply floating on top of the swamp. When stepped on, the ground can be felt moving, hence the reason Native Americans called the swamp 'Land of the Trembling Earth'.

The U.S. Fish and Wildlife Service, with the help of volunteers, have constructed many overnight shelters that are accessible by canoe or kayak. The shelters must be reserved in advance and are typically reached via a six to twelve-mile paddle. Over the course of eleven separate trips, I have kayaked to and camped at six of these shelters.

All the shelters are constructed in the same manner with the exception of one, which is an old hunting cabin located on a small island in the center of the swamp. The other shelters are built directly over the water or peat moss and resemble a large deck. Half of the deck is covered by a roof, with four open sides, and the other half is open to the sky; there is a vault toilet located at each shelter, as well as a picnic table.

***

The most precarious situation I encountered over the many trips to the swamp was an event I had never considered would occur and, therefore, I had not prepared for. I was kayaking with two others on that trip, including my brother Christopher. Starting at Stephen Foster State Park, we paddled eleven miles to the Big Water shelter, a paddle none of us had ever attempted.

Similar to paddling to other shelters in the swamp, we had one location on the entire paddle to get out of our kayaks, stretch our legs, and take a bathroom break. Otherwise, there was no dry land, meaning we were stuck in our kayaks unless we wanted to swim in waist-deep, alligator-infested water. On this particular trip, we spotted around a hundred alligators, most over six-foot in length, which instilled a strong desire to avoid getting in the water.

After a few hours of paddling, we arrived at the Big Water shelter and began unloading our gear. My kayak had a dry storage compartment where I kept most of my camping gear. The compartment ensured my essential gear, including extra clothes and sleeping bag, would stay dry. But when I opened the compartment, I was alarmed to see my gear sitting in a few inches of water. Everything in the compartment including my sleeping bag and extra clothes were soaked. And even more worrisome was the fact that I had a hole in my kayak.

My first priority was to get the kayak out of the water and onto the shelter platform. Then, I knew my sleeping bag needed to dry out as soon as possible. The overnight temperature was expected to be in the forties, which would make for a cold night without a sleeping bag. With only a couple hours of daylight left, I promptly opened the sleeping bag and hung it from the shelter ceiling to air dry.

My attention then turned towards the kayak. A quick inspection revealed a hole in the keel (the bottom center of the stern). Many thoughts raced through my head, such as 'How do I fix it?' and 'How do I get back to the car if I can't fix it?'. We were eleven miles from the boat landing and just as far from any cell phone service. If I could not fix the leak, then Christopher and my friend would have to leave me the next day to get help, meaning we'd be in the swamp until at least late the next day. With severe thunderstorms forecasted for the following afternoon, we wanted to avoid that option at all costs.

I never imagined or prepared for a hole in my kayak while paddling on flat water. It would have been a different story if we had been traveling through rapids and rocky terrain, but being in the swamp, I never considered the situation.

Christopher, on the other hand, had prepared for such an occurrence, and pulled out a tube of marine grade silicone from his bag. We used the silicone to fill the hole and hopefully stop the leak, but with hours of drying time needed, I would not be able to test it until the next morning. With the kayak situation taken care of, we set up camp and enjoyed the sunset.

That evening we were fortunate to hear what I'd say is the most primeval sound in nature. The first time we heard it, we all froze and looked at each other, seeking confirmation that someone else heard the noise as well. It sounded as if a large predator was growling at us, like what I'd imagine a dinosaur would sound like. We had just begun frying some hushpuppies prior to hearing the sound, so I thought the smell must have attracted a hungry predator.

The hair stood up on the back of my neck and an eerie feeling came across my body. None of us said a word, and then a few seconds later we heard it again. We began speculating what it could be, and then shined our flashlights through the swamp in an attempt to spot the creature.

I knew Florida Panthers (similar to a mountain lion) had been spotted before in the swamp and that many black bears inhabited the area, so I was certain a panther or bear was stalking us, yet we could not spot any eyes reflecting in our light beams.

Then, we heard a second creature produce the same noise, this time very close to and directly in front of our shelter. Shining our flashlights in the area, we noticed an alligator floating in the water, and while watching the alligator, we witnessed it produce the sound we were hearing.

It was such a relief knowing we were not being stalked by a panther or bear but were instead listening to an alligator bellowing. For the rest of the evening, we enjoyed the primeval sounds of the swamp and felt like we had been taken back in time to the Jurassic period.

The next morning, I placed my kayak into the water and inspected the patch job. It appeared to be holding well, so we loaded up and commenced our eleven-mile paddle back to the car. The entire paddle I thought of what I would do if I started to sink, of which I never came up with a good plan. There was no dry land and we were seeing alligators every few minutes, so I just paddled faster, eager to get back to dry land.

The last half mile we got caught in the rain, and then soon after getting to our car, a severe thunderstorm warning was issued over the swamp. We got out just in time, all thanks to Christopher's insight to bring marine grade silicone on the trip.

Camp set-up on the Big Water shelter

THE UNEXPLAINED

Floyd's Island, located deep in the interior of the Okefenokee, is home to my favorite shelter: An old hunting cabin built in the 1920's, absent of electricity, running water, or furniture. Arriving at the island is like traveling back in time a hundred years, and the hundred acres of dry land that make up the island provide ample room to explore.

I researched many historical reports prior to the trip and learned about the vast history of the island. Previous inhabitants included numerous Indian tribes and other prior civilizations, such as the Weeden Island Culture which existed over 1,500 years ago.

The last known civilization to inhabit the land, before General Charles Rinaldo Floyd discovered the island while carrying out duties to remove Indians from the area, were the Seminoles. After General Floyd burnt down the abandoned Seminole village in 1838, the island was named Floyd's Island.

I have completed two trips to the island, both with very memorable encounters. The first was with my brother Christopher and my friend Rocky. After completing multiple Okefenokee wilderness trips together in the past, we wanted to stay at a shelter with room to walk around and with an area to build a fire, so our best option was the island.

With our kayaks loaded down with camping gear and a lot of cooking supplies, such as charcoal and a grill grate, we started our eight-mile paddle to the island. The first half of the paddle was up a winding river through large cyprus stands, while the last few miles followed a shallow and narrow creek through heavy scrub brush and forest.

When we arrived at the island, we unloaded our gear and explored the surrounding area, taking notice of some interesting rock mounds to the east of the cabin. The area immediately surrounding the cabin was filled with old growth oak trees, and then a little further out were areas of tall pines. We walked about ten or fifteen minutes north of the cabin to a clearing, and then worked our way back to the cabin, seeing many deer, squirrels, and armadillos along the way.

Since the weather was forecasted to be nice that evening, our plan was to sleep in a tent just outside the cabin. But as we continued to explore the surrounding area, we began to experience an uneasy feeling. The ambiance of the island spooked us a bit, with the Spanish moss, the rock mounds, the brutal history of the area, the eerie quiet, and the isolation. As a result, we slowly talked ourselves into sleeping inside the cabin due to the strange and uneasy feeling we had.

There were two entries into the cabin, both through doors with interior latches. Inside the cabin were four rooms, and between each room was a door with a latch.

Based on my experience with backpacking shelters I knew there would probably be mice in the cabin, and where there are mice there are usually snakes. Therefore, I suggested we pitch the tent inside the cabin to provide protection from the mice, snakes, spiders, scorpions, and other insects, which Christopher and Rocky agreed.

Back outside and having packed a soft-sided cooler, a small bag of charcoal, and a metal grill grate, we built a fire and prepared dinner. It took thirty minutes to cook our thick ribeye steaks over the fire, which filled the air with a pleasant aroma. We ate our steaks under the moonlight, along with potato chips and other numerous snacks.

The rest of the evening we sat around and talked for hours next to our large, bright, and warm fire. A few times we heard noises coming from the woods, but we brushed them off as being either a racoon, an armadillo, or a deer, as we had already seen all those animals since arriving on the island.

Around 10:00 P.M., we made our way inside the cabin and into our tent. With all our food inside the cabin, we secured the latches on each door to prevent any pesky racoons or bears from wandering inside looking for a quick snack.

The room was pitch-black when we turned off our headlamps. Even after giving our eyes time to adjust to the dark, we still could not see more than a few inches in front of our face. So I closed my eyes and tried to fall asleep to what I thought was going to be a restful night.

Floyd's Cabin

I woke up a few times during the night. The first time was due to a noise coming from inside our room, but outside the tent. I had a small, soft-sided cooler inside the room, which I was sure I had fully zipped up. Yet the sound of an animal drinking out of the cooler, similar to a dog drinking out of a bowl, filled the air.

I looked through the mesh of the tent, but it was too dark to see anything, and I did not want to turn on my flashlight, as it would have awoken the other guys. I could not think of any way an animal large enough to produce the noise could be inside the room, as we had latched all the doors. But the noise stopped less than a minute later, so I choose to just ignore it and go back to sleep.

The sound of something walking back and forth on the front deck woke me the second time. Not only could I hear it walking, but I could also hear it breathing, and it sounded large. A recent camper wrote in the cabin logbook that they saw a black bear nearby, so my best guess of the creature's identity was a black bear, attracted to the cabin by the smell of our food. With both exterior doors securely latched, I went back to sleep with little concern.

A few hours later I woke up for the third time. My eyes were closed, but I noticed it was no longer dark inside the tent. Opening my eyes expecting to see sunlight coming through the cabin window, I instead saw Christopher sitting up on one knee, his headlamp on, holding his pistol, and looking out the mesh of the tent towards the backdoor of the room.

My adrenaline shot up, and immediately I was wide awake. I had no idea what was happening and whispered to him, asking what was going on. He responded, "Someone is in the other room."

We were literally in the middle of nowhere, with the only access to the island being an eight-mile canoe trail from one direction, and a thirteen-mile canoe trail from the other. If there was someone else here, in our cabin, at 4:00 A.M., sneaking around quietly, then we had a problem.

We sat there, completely still and focused on the door. Many minutes went by, but there were no sounds to be heard except for Rocky snoring. I looked at Christopher, and suggested it was probably a deer or some other animal on the back deck, and for him to go back to sleep.

I had already laid back down and closed my eyes when I finally heard it: I heard footsteps coming from the adjacent room, undeniably human like footsteps, causing the old wood floor to creak. My heart started beating faster as I opened my eyes, sat up, and now grabbed my pistol too.

We stared at the door, waiting for it to open and for someone to walk in. We whispered to each other, speculating if it could it be anything other than a person, and how anything could have made its way inside as we had latched the exterior doors and all the windows were intact.

For the next fifteen minutes we sat there and listened, hearing the footsteps every so often. If it were a person, we did not want to yell out, as obviously they were attempting to go unnoticed.

Out of nowhere, Rocky woke up and let out a loud outburst after seeing us sitting up, with our headlamps on, and our guns in our hand. We looked at him and told him to shut up because there was someone in the other room. Suddenly, Rocky's eyes grew really wide, really quick, and he was now alert and staring at the door.

But after Rocky's loud outburst, the noises ceased, and just like I had done earlier without actually hearing the noise, he suggested it must have been an animal on the back deck and that we were overreacting.

It was now around 5:00 A.M. and Christopher needed to go to the bathroom. The privy at this location was a long way from the cabin. A trail through the woods about 100 to 150 yards long led to the vault toilet. Christopher did not want to walk there alone and for good reason, thinking whoever or whatever we heard in the adjacent room was now just outside the cabin. Rocky was ready to fall back asleep and did not want to leave his warm sleeping bag, so he called Christopher a wuss and told him to go alone.

I had a little more sympathy for Christopher and agreed to walk with him. Rocky saw us unzip the tent and both step out, in which he shot up and said, "Oh heck no, you're not leaving me here alone." We then all walked through the woods together at 5:00 A.M. just so Christopher did not have to go to the bathroom alone.

Daybreak appeared not long after, and we spent some time investigating the noises. All the cabin doors were still latched, windows secured, and there were no holes in the floor or ceiling, meaning there was no way the noise could have come from a large animal inside the cabin.

We walked around in the other room, simulating the sounds a human would make; it sounded exactly like the sounds we heard that night.

The cooler I had next to the tent, the one I heard an animal drinking out of, was zipped closed. No animal in the swamp could possibly unzip the cooler, drink out of it, and then zip it back up.

Our investigation made us even more uneasy about the previous night, and we wasted no time packing up our kayaks and getting off the island that morning.

Reflecting on that night, I still do not know what produced the noises we heard. Christopher is convinced it was another person. While I don't have a good argument with him based on what I heard, I believe it was supernatural.

As mentioned before, the island was home to many prior civilizations, including an American Indian village pushed out forcefully and burned by settlers.

Archaeological reports have identified burial mounds on the island and elsewhere in the swamp, and suggest they were present long before the Seminole Indians inhabited the area. Experts speculate the remains are from the Weeden Island culture, who inhabited the island at some point before the Seminoles.

Throughout the history of the swamp, many supernatural encounters have been reported. The way the night's events played out and from what our investigation found the next morning, I have no other explanation for the noises other than it was some sort of spirit.

One thing this trip highlighted was the potential for encounters with both people and animals, and the potential need to protect yourself. I always carry a firearm, where legal, when I am in the wilderness. There is no 911 and no contact with help in many places in the wilderness, including the swamp. If we were in a situation where someone or something wanted to harm us, we would need to defend ourselves without relying on any outside help.

I have never needed to use a firearm for self-defense, but I do not ever want to be in a situation where I need one and do not have it. When it comes to wildlife such as bears, I am a strong believer in using bear spray rather than a firearm, but I also do not believe bears are nearly as great of a threat than other humans are.

Hundreds of crimes are committed each year in National Parks, including many assaults, kidnappings, and murders. Ever since the federal law was changed in 2010 to allow concealed carry of firearms in national parks, I always carry mine.

WILDLIFE

Park regulations require launching a canoe or kayak no later than 10:00 A.M. when completing an overnight trip. In order to avoid a long and early morning drive to the launch site from our homes four hours away, we have always chosen to camp near the swamp the night before our paddle.

There are three entrances into the swamp for launching a wilderness kayaking trip. One of these entrances, Stephen Foster State Park, offers a very nice campground with water, electricity, bath houses, and a general store. Wanting to stay in the state park campground prior to our 9th trip into the swamp, we only had a few options of shelters to choose from, one of which was Floyd's Island, and so it became our shelter of choice for the trip.

The paddle in for our second trip to Floyd's Island was long and uneventful. When we arrived at the island, I was anxious to get out and walk around, having been cooped up in my kayak for hours. But before unloading our gear, I wanted to take some pictures of us at the landing.

To get a picture of all three of us, our kayaks, and the general background, I needed to prop my cell phone camera onto something. There was a very large stump next to the landing that looked perfect for propping up my phone.

I tried many spots on the stump, moving higher and lower, trying to get the right angle. After at least two minutes of trying to set up my camera phone, I saw the most freighting thing less than a foot away from my hand. My heart skipped a beat, and I jumped back quicker than I ever have in my life, dropping my phone on the ground and practically tripping over my own feet.

Christopher and my friend looked at me like I was crazy. I pointed at the stump and yelled "snake!" My hand had been less than a foot from the rattle of a six-foot-long Timber rattlesnake.

The highly poisonous snake did not move nor rattle. After I calmed my nerves, we unloaded our gear while observing the snake from a safe distance. It was January, and the temperature was in the fifties, most likely explaining the snake's sluggish nature. Reading the logbook at the cabin, many recent guests reported seeing the same snake at the same location. While we were slightly concerned it may slither its way over to our camp a hundred yards away, we did not think it was likely due to the cold weather. And sure enough, it was sitting on the same stump, though in a different location, the following morning.

I thought a lot about what to do if one of us was bitten by the snake. Paddling out would take three or four hours, and with no dry land, it would not be smart to paddle after being bit; if you pass out in a kayak with no dry land around, the gravity of the situation would be magnified. However, paddling out would have been the only real option we had unless we successfully reached someone via my VHF radio or received a successful transmission signal on my personal satellite distress beacon.

For treating an actual bite there are many methods about what to do. Recent studies have suggested that there are no known clinically proven treatments that can be performed in the field, and the number one priority is to get the patient to a hospital where antivenom can be administered. During transport keep the limb at the same level as the heart. Do not apply a tourniquet, do not suck the venom out, and do not try to apply electricity to the wound. Some evidence suggests a benefit when using pressure bandages for certain types of snake bites (those with neurotoxins).

***

Over 10,000 alligators are estimated to live in the Okefenokee, and each trip I have taken to the swamp resulted in spotting anywhere from 5 to 200 alligators. While any alligator has the potential to be dangerous and even deadly to humans, the fact is attacks are extremely rare and are usually a result of a careless human. Since 1980, only one person has been killed by an alligator in Georgia.

Alligators are most active and in search of food during the hot summer weather. Once the temperature drops into the sixties, an alligator will cease to hunt; and then once the temperature drops into the mid-fifties, it will become very sluggish and dormant in an attempt to retain body heat. Since most of our trips into the swamp occur in the fall and winter, when temperatures are fifty degrees or less, we typically spot many sluggish alligators sunbathing on the shore in an attempt to keep warm.

Christopher, Rocky, another friend, and I paddled to the Round Top shelter in early October when the temperature was still eighty degrees. The enhanced activity of the alligators from the warm weather was very apparent.

Just a few miles into our paddle, there was a group of five to six large alligators swimming back and forth across the canal. We maintained course on the large waterway and started to paddle through the congregation, when

59

suddenly one of the alligators swam directly towards Christopher. The alligator approached quickly and was so close that Christopher had to raise his paddle out of the water as to not hit the alligator.

The alligator then swung its tail heavily into the backside of Christopher's kayak, rocking his kayak so much that water almost spilled in over the side. Never having seen this level of aggression before, we quickly paddled further upstream.

The remainder of the paddle to the shelter, along with our evening, was uneventful. Then the next morning, we began our paddle back to the landing. The Round Top shelter was located a few miles off the main canal and was only accessible via a narrow canoe trail, with many sections of this trail being so narrow that it was difficult to paddle without hitting brush.

Christopher was in the lead, followed by me, Rocky, and our other friend. We were about a mile into the paddle when Christopher stopped. He had spotted an alligator in front of him, but I was not sure why he was stopping. We had seen so many alligators that we had stop paying much attention to them anymore. I called out and told him to keep moving, in which he responded he could not.

It turned out the alligator either would not or could not submerge in the shallow water, and with the narrow path, there was no option to get around him safely. We were stuck at a stalemate for many minutes, unsure about how to continue.

Eventually, Christopher began slowly moving towards the alligator, and got within inches of him; so close he could have touched him with his hand. The alligator had his mouth wide open and was hissing, something we had never seen.

Suddenly, the alligator bit down, swiped his tail, and took off underneath Christopher's kayak, causing the kayak to rock heavily. A second or two later, I felt a large bump hit the bottom of my kayak; and then so did Rocky and our other friend. We were now safe from the alligator, but our nerves were all shot.

To this day, we still do not know what else we could have done to safely get past the alligator without harassing it. We did not want to throw anything at him or splash water on him, but we could not sit there all day either. The situation played itself out for the better, but I hope we never have an encounter like that again.

***

While this next story did not occur in the Okefenokee, it did involve an alligator in nearby Northern Florida. Christopher and I were on a SCUBA trip to check out a few of the natural springs that are abundant across the northern section of Florida, including Alexander Springs.

The crystal clear and shallow Alexander Springs serves as a popular swimming hole for many locals and for the guests of the park's campground. We hauled our SCUBA gear over to the edge and began getting ready for our dive, when a couple of people warned us there was an alligator in the water. Without much concern, we jumped into the water and started our dive.

The majority of the dive site was only ten feet in depth with a lot of vegetation growing from the sandy bottom. The natural spring feeding the area created the most impressive feature of the dive, a twenty to twenty-five-foot-deep impression absent of any vegetation. All around this void were many large fish, about one-foot long, and almost solid black, known as Plecos.

Sitting almost perfectly still on the downslope of the impression was a six-foot long alligator. The alligator was not paying us any attention, so we sat on the bottom about thirty feet away and watched him for a few minutes. The alligator sat still until a Pleco swam within striking distance, in which he lurched forward in an attempt to secure a meal. We watched the alligator do this many times unsuccessfully, and then we continued our dive around the spring.

Back on dry land, we broke down our gear after the relatively uneventful dive. Another pair of divers walked up to us and asked if we had any issues with the alligator. After relaying our not too exciting observations, one of the other divers told us they had just completed their dive when we were starting ours, and that their dive was a lot more eventful.

Just like us, they had observed the alligator for a few minutes before continuing through the spring. Shortly after turning their backs on the alligator, one of the divers suddenly felt something tugging on his fin as if another diver had grabbed it to get his attention. When he turned around, the alligator was right there, with his jaws locked down on his fin. The diver, using a large underwater camera, began banging the alligators head, but it would not let go. Then, the diver inadvertently triggered the flash on his camera, which spooked the alligator enough to release its death grip and swim off.

While we all discussed the incident, it was apparent what had happened. The alligator had been hunting the Plecos when we observed it, and taking a look at our solid black fins, we noticed the resemblance between the fins and the Plecos. The alligator most likely mistook the diver's fin as a Pleco. Thankfully, everyone ended up okay, and we were able to go about our vacation and dive at some other sites.

NEW PERSPECTIVES

Kayak camping in the swamp affords a great opportunity to introduce wilderness camping to others. The most common mistake made by first-time wilderness campers is they pack too much gear. While very disadvantageous while backpacking, over packing isn't a large hinderance while kayaking, making kayak camping a great introduction to wilderness camping.

One year, Christopher, Rocky, and I invited four others to join us on our annual Okefenokee trip; however, we would be kayaking and camping just outside of the National Wildlife Refuge this time. Of the four new additions, the least experienced person had never been wilderness camping before, and the most experienced person had recently completed a multi-day backcountry hunting trip in New Zealand.

With the wide range of experience and backgrounds, I knew this trip would not only serve to teach others about wilderness camping skills, but that I would learn things too. I had been to the swamp many times prior to this trip and had my own perspective of the swamp, the paddle, and the necessary gear and supplies; the dos and don'ts had already been engrained in me, shaped from the bias of always completing the trip with the same group of people.

My friend Eryc, who I had known for about fifteen years, was joining us on the trip. We had hunted and camped together in high school over ten years prior, so I was looking forward to him coming on the trip. He was an avid hunter with experience ranging from big game hunting in New Zealand, to alligator hunting in South Carolina. He was also an avid fisherman, great with a rod and reel, but also proficient in spearfishing while freediving.

When we arrived at the boat landing early Saturday morning, I helped everyone load gear into their kayaks and get them on the water. Most of the gear was what I expected to see: tents, sleeping bags, dry bags full of gear, and food. A few folks loaded fishing poles, but Eryc took it a step further with enough tackle for a full-fledged fishing excursion. Then, I saw him and others loading up a frying pan, a large gas camping stove, a pack of flour, salt/pepper, plates, oil, etc. It looked like they were going on a multi-day expedition! I tilted my head and gave them a 'what are you thinking' look, and without the need to say anything, Eryc replied in his confidence of eating fresh fish that night.

I packed extra food like I do with every trip, but this time I was pretty sure it would all be consumed by Eryc. Of all the trips we had taken to the swamp previously, we had not caught a single fish, and I had no confidence they would catch any.

Our paddle to the campsite was the shortest I had done in or around the swamp, taking no more than a few hours. After setting up camp, Eryc and a few others pulled out their fishing poles and wetted their lines. The first hour or two was exactly like I expected, not a single bite, but I could see their determination to catch a fish and knew they would not give up until successful. About an hour before sunset was when it finally happened, and I had to admit I was impressed with the few fish they caught.

Soon after, the frogs sprung to life and the sounds of the swamp echoed off the water. Eryc became wide-eyed and immediately shifted gears from fishing to hunting mode. He was bound and determined to catch a frog and feast on frog legs for dinner. I laughed, knowing there was no possible way we would catch these frogs; we were surrounded by swamp, it was cold, and none of us had waders, so unless the frog was right next to our small piece of dry land, we would have to frog hunt from our unstable kayaks.

The first fifteen minutes of frog hunting were comical. Eryc and a couple others tried their best to catch a frog by hand while sitting in their kayak, but it was just not happening. A few times they would briefly wrap their hands around a frog, but they could not hold on.

Eryc paddled back to camp and went through his tackle box, pulling out five large hooks. He then straightened out the hooks so each one resembled a tiny spear. Borrowing a cane fishing pole (a long bamboo cane), he fastened the hooks to the end of the pole and essentially created a homemade frog gig.

The sun had now set, and everyone donned their headlamps. Setting out again in his kayak, Eryc quickly spotted many frogs close by. Ever so slowly he paddled within striking distance of a frog. He raised the newly assembled gig, slowly inching it closer to the frog. Then with a swift strike, he successfully hit and secured our first frog.

This same routine went on for about an hour, and with all of us partaking in the hunt, resulted in the capture of about fifteen to twenty frogs. I could not believe we really just caught enough frogs and fish to feed everyone that evening.

We enjoyed a hot, fresh, and delicious dinner in the middle of nowhere that night. It is not often that I am as content as I was then; sitting in the middle of a swamp with a group of friends, miles away from civilization, frying fresh frog legs and fish filets, learning new wilderness skills, and having added to my knowledge of kayak camping in the swamp. Thankfully, my pessimistic opinion about catching food for dinner was proven wrong.

That evening my mind wondered about what the right way is to plan for, execute, and safely enjoy a wilderness trip: if I plan on catching or hunting for my meal on the next trip rather than packing food, but end up getting skunked, the results of that failure would be uncomfortable, yet I'd probably still survive. If the end goal is to survive while fully experiencing the wilderness, with the now proven prospect of enjoying an amazing meal sourced in the wild, then why not take the chance?

I thought again of why I go on these trips: To experience nature and solitude, and to be presented with the challenges of being away from the everyday things that make us comfortable, the things that people take for granted and think are guaranteed. By not packing food and challenging myself to source food from the land, wouldn't this achieve my desire?

Ultimately, I still pack enough food to get through a trip comfortably, but will at least prepare for and try to source fresh food from the land.

I am thankful we expanded our group and invited others on the trip. As mentioned before, there is no better time to try something new than the present. Eryc passed away less than six months after the trip; if we had postponed or cancelled due to the cold December weather that year, or just did not invite all the people we did, then his influences, knowledge, and experiences would have never been shared with us.

SWAMP PLANNING

Planning and packing for an overnight kayak trip in the

swamp requires a different mindset than preparing for a backpacking trip in the mountains.

Packing for kayak camping is a lot simpler than for backpacking. Kayaks have plenty of room to store gear, including non-essential items, and packing a few extra pounds is not a hindrance. While packing, I always start with the essentials, placing them into one pile, while placing all the non-essential gear into a separate pile.

This ability to pack almost everything we could possibly need has proven helpful in a few situations and has also made each trip more enjoyable since we could pack more snacks and a variety of beverages.

Essentials in the swamp include a tent or a hammock with a bug net, even if the plan is to sleep outside under the stars, as weather and bug activity can be hard to predict. A sleeping pad is essential for me, though I am sure there are some who enjoy sleeping directly on a wood floor. A sleeping bag or a blanket is always on my list, and since I have room in my kayak, I always pack a pillow, even though it is not essential.

I bring at least a gallon of water per night, and just in case of an emergency, I pack some water purification tablets.

If I am staying at one of the few shelters that allow fires, I coordinate with my camping partners and pack a shared dinner consisting of some meat in a small, soft-sided cooler, along with a small amount of charcoal and a cooking grate. Otherwise, I will pack either a freeze-dried meal or pasta, and then I always have trail mix, granola, and energy bars for breakfast and lunch.

A change of clothes packed into a dry bag is essential since water is always in close proximity, especially in the winter when hypothermia can occur quickly.

Other essential gear includes a map (with topo and

aerial imagery), compass, first aid kit, life jacket, noise making device (a whistle or airhorn), knife, flashlight, sunscreen, bug spray, VHF radio, rope, toilet paper, lighter or matches, and something to patch a small hole in your boat.

When all the essential gear has been packed and loaded, I go to my non-essential pile and see what I still have room for. Junk food is always great in the backcountry, like cookies and candy, which really are not that bad for you considering the number of calories burned paddling.

We pack at least one fishing pole between everyone going on the trip, unless we are staying on Floyd's Island where there are no areas to fish. After the trip with Eryc, we ended up catching fish on the next trip, and since we had packed a pan with a small amount of oil and flour, we had a fantastic meal that night.

Pre-planning for emergencies while in the swamp, when the only access is by boat, is different than backpacking. The best means of self-rescue is by your own kayak, especially in the winter where walking in the water could induce hypothermia. I always have rope in case we need to tow someone in their kayak, either due to a lost paddle, injury, or illness.

For situations where it is not possible to self-rescue, I always pack a VHF radio and satellite distress beacon to call for help. Lastly, I always study and attempt to memorize maps and aerial imagery before the trip, which could prove helpful if we get off course while paddling.

5 - THE HARSH ENVIRONMENT

SNOW

It was the end of October 2014 and I was meeting my friend Josh for our first backpacking trip together. He had completed some solo backpacking trips over the past few years, so his backpacking experience was greater than mine. Josh had taken the whole week off work and was attempting to hike the entire Appalachian Trail (AT) section of Great Smoky Mountains National Park (GSMNP).

I could not take the entire week off, so the plan was to meet near the halfway point and complete the second half together. Starting Saturday morning at Fontana Dam and hiking north to Newfound Gap, Josh would be faced with roughly forty miles of trail and almost 13,000 feet of combined elevation gain before meeting me.

The plan was to meet Josh on Wednesday with his resupplies, and then continue northbound to the park boundary at Davenport Gap; a 30.5-mile hike with 8,400 feet of elevation gain. At Davenport Gap, we had a shuttle scheduled to pick us up around noon on Saturday. This meant we needed supplies for at least four days and three nights, plus emergency supplies for one extra day.

Below is our itinerary put together a few weeks before the trip:

AT Hike 10/25 -11/1

Fontana Dam to Davenport Gap – Smoky Mountains National Park.

Sat 10/25 – Fontana Dam to Mollies Ridge

Sun 10/26 – Mollies Ridge to Derrick Knob

Mon 10/27 – Derrick Knob to Double Spring Gap

Tue 10/28 – Double Spring to Mt. Collins

Wed 10/29 – Mt. Collins to Ice Water Spring: Colby Farrow joins at Newfound Gap

Thurs 10/30 – Ice Water to Tri Corner

Fri – 10/31 – Tri Corner to Cosby Knob

Sat – 11/1 – Cosby Knob to Davenport Gap: Shuttle back to Colby's truck at Newfound Gap.

When backpacking the AT through GSMNP, with the exception of AT thru-hikers, hikers are required to reserve a spot in one of the primitive shelters. Pitching a tent off the trail or even next to a shelter was prohibited for all non-thru-hikers. This made planning and logistics more important, as we had to choose a specific shelter for each night, weeks before the trip.

Staying in a shelter had its downsides and its perks. Without the need to pack a tent, about five pounds of pack weight and a lot of pack space would be saved; and there would be no additional time spent setting up and breaking down a tent each day.

We knew the shelters in GSMNP were some of the best on the entire AT, most with enough room for at least eight people to sleep comfortably. They were enclosed on three sides with an open face, usually facing the leeward side of the mountain, and all had very reliable roofs. Each shelter had a bench area to sit down and prepare meals, eat, and just relax, along with a composting privy.

Most importantly, given the approximately 1,500 bears that live in the park, bear cables were provided at each shelter to store food out of the reach of any hungry bear. On Josh's second night, before I joined him, he was awoken to a bear trying to get his food bag from the cables. After about ten minutes, the bear gave up and walked away.

The downsides to staying in a shelter include the ever-present mice and the potential to have fellow campers with you. While I enjoy talking to and sharing stories with others, you just never know who is going to show up. I go into the wilderness to seek solitude and quietness, and to enjoy nature and its tranquility, not to potentially spend an evening with someone who is loud or obnoxious, stays up a lot later than me, or is a loud snorer.

I had acquired a lot of new backpacking gear and felt very prepared for the multi-night trek. I had a new sleeping bag, a new backpack, a new water bottle filter, and new lightweight cookware. After loading my pack with all my gear, it only weighed around thirty to thirty-five pounds. I felt confident in the hike and was more than ready to face whatever the trail presented.

***

Josh walked off the trail and into the parking lot at Newfound Gap late Wednesday morning, which was crowded with tourists enjoying the fall season. The temperature was in the forties and the wind was fairly light, and for the most part, it was overcast skies with a light mist.

We double checked the weather forecast in the parking lot, knowing this may be the last time we would have cell phone service. The forecast each night showed temperatures in the upper teens to low twenties, and there was a slight chance of snow on Friday and Saturday.

This did not really concern us. It was late October and most snow events that time of year are very light, with maybe one or two inches maximum. So, we pressed ahead with our itinerary as scheduled and headed north on the AT.

The trail immediately headed uphill on a moderately difficult and heavily trafficked path. The elevation went from 5,046 feet at the parking lot, to near 6,000 feet along the three-mile trek to our first shelter, Icewater Spring. The shelter was large, in great shape, and had an amazing view overlooking the park. The shelter was strategically placed slightly lower than the summit and on the east side, which was the leeward side of the mountain; protecting us from the prevailing winds.

There were no other people when we arrived at the shelter. After setting up our beds and unpacking our gear, we relaxed and enjoyed the view on a brisk, fall afternoon.

Over the next few hours, three more hikers arrived at the shelter with intentions of staying the night, one being a southbound thru-hiker. We sat around and talked for a while, and then cooked our dinner. I had a freeze-dried Mountain House meal, some trail mix, and hot tea.

The Icewater Spring shelter had a fireplace incorporated into the rock structure. We were not too cold but went ahead and tried to build a fire. The damp wood was difficult to light, and after thirty to forty-five minutes of failed attempts, we gave up. The fire was not a necessity; we had a shelter, warm clothes, and sleeping bags, but the effort to get it burning kept us all entertained for a while.

Everyone got into their sleeping bags around 9:00 P.M. when the temperature starting plummeting. The day before the trip, I made the decision to pack my new zero-degree sleeping bag instead of my twenty-degree bag, as the forecast called for low temperatures in the mid-teens. I stayed very warm all night, and actually woke up sweating in my sleeping bag; I had to let some of the freezing cold air into my bag to cool me off. I do not regret bringing that bag however, as Josh brought a twenty-degree bag and ended up very cold that night, and as he would describe, was the coldest night of his life.

***

Ice covered the ground when we woke Thursday morning shortly before dawn. There was no precipitation overnight, but rather the ice was a result of heavy frost from the calm, moist air.

Having a weak cell phone signal, we checked the weather again, taking a keen interest in the updated snow forecast. The update showed a 50% chance of snow Friday night and Saturday, with two to four inches of accumulation possible. We discussed the situation over breakfast and determined that we had the appropriate gear to continue on, and if needed, hike through a few inches of snow on Saturday.

When the sun appeared over the mountain lined horizon, the rays glistened off the ice and provided much needed warmth. We loaded up our gear and prepared to hike to the next shelter, refilling our water from a nearby natural spring.

I used my new backpacking water filter, even though the water was coming straight out of the ground. I always err on the side of caution when it comes to drinking water in the wilderness, and either use a filter device or purification tablets. Contracting a virus or bacteria from untreated water is easily avoidable by taking a few extra minutes to use this common-sense technique.

Knowing there would be opportunities to refill water every few miles based on our trail guides, we both carried around two liters of water (about four pounds) in an effort to minimize pack weight.

Refilling my water for the first time, I quickly learned I had packed the wrong type of water filter for this trip. I had a water bottle that had a built-in filter. To operate the filter, about twelve ounces of water could be placed in the bottle at a time, and then the bottle had to be squeezed forcefully to push the water through the filter.

The process was extremely slow, taking a few minutes per each twelve ounces of water. With the need to fill up two liters at a time, I was stuck forcefully squeezing and filtering water for a good fifteen minutes. If we had been in an area that contained more risky water, then the added benefit of the virus filter on my device would have been worth the extra effort. But with water coming straight out of the ground, a simple gravity filter to protect against bacteria and protozoa was all we needed.

Soon after completing the trip, I purchased a gravity fed filter device that could filter a liter of water in just a minute or two, and without any forced assistance.

***

The plan for day two (day six for Josh) was to hike from Icewater Spring to Tricorner Knob. The distance between the shelters was roughly 12.5 miles, with many sustained climbs of 800+ feet along the way. For the most part, the trail stayed between 5,000 and 6,000 feet, and followed a spectacular ridgeline on the Tennessee/North Carolina border.

The first mile was downhill and led us to the best view east of the Mississippi, Charlie's Bunion. I would have stayed there all day if time allowed. We spent at least thirty minutes admiring the view of spectacular cliffs and the Tennessee Valley, and I must have taken over a hundred pictures. I made a mental note to come back in the future on a day trip, as reaching this overlook from the main parking area can be done as a moderately-strenuous day hike, with about eight miles roundtrip of hiking and 1,600 feet of elevation gain.

I was both physically and mentally content when we pushed on to Tricorner Knob. Passing about ten other people during the hike, we ended up having the same conversation about the incoming weather system. Cell phone service was non-existent after leaving Icewater Spring that morning, so our only source of information was from other hikers. We brushed off the more severe warnings from a few folks as we assumed these hikers saw the same forecast we had seen a few hours earlier, and we continued our hike forward. After a long and tough day of hiking, we made it to the shelter and joined two other people already there.

We all talked about the impending weather. The other hikers started at Davenport Gap (where we had planned to end our hike) and they were planning on hiking the next day in the direction Josh and I had come from. On their hike up earlier in the day, they came across a trail runner who gave them an updated forecast, and apparently the snow chance had increased to over 75%, and the accumulation increased to upwards of four to eight inches.

Soon after we cooked dinner, an AT thru-hiker arrived at the shelter. He had hiked over twenty-five miles that day and had an even more grim prognosis of the weather. He last saw a forecast of over twelve inches of snow and the potential for blizzard conditions beginning the following afternoon.

The new information immediately created concern. Our plan for Friday (the following day) was to hike seven miles to Cosby Knob, and then hike another nine miles Saturday to the highway where a shuttle was scheduled to pick us up at noon. If we stuck to this plan, we could potentially have to hike in over twelve inches of snow, in blizzard like conditions, and down a steep 3,000-foot descent on Saturday.

The shuttle was another concern, as we felt it may not be capable of picking us up in those conditions; and we had no cell service, with no guarantee we would have service at the trail exit either.

Knowing we did not have the skills or equipment necessary to hike in those conditions, and with the potential to be stranded for a day or more, we knew we had to get off the trail the following day. The other two hikers at the shelter, as well as the thru hiker, came to the same conclusion.

Josh and I spent the next couple of hours thinking of our best option to get off the trail before the storm hit. Our current location was almost exactly the halfway point between the parking lot at Newfound Gap, and the highway at Davenport Gap, with only nature existing between the two. Basically, we had to make the decision to hike to one of those two locations.

We pulled out the topo map and assessed the hike to Davenport Gap, which neither of us had ever done, and then compared that assessment with our previous two days of hiking from Newfound Gap. We also conferred with the pair of hikers that came from Davenport Gap that day.

If we chose to hike to Davenport Gap, we would be faced with a 15.3-mile trek that was mostly downhill. Overall, there would be over 7,000 feet in descent and 3,200 feet in ascent. Two options existed on how to get to Davenport Gap, one being on the AT, and the other via two side trails that drop quickly into a valley, then follow a creek down to the gap. This option appeared slightly shorter and with less undulating elevation, and theoretically would receive less snow than the high ridges.

If we arrived at Davenport Gap Friday, we would need to figure out a way back to our car at Newfound Gap. That was the biggest unknown, and a variable we could not control. As much as we wanted to check off this remote and difficult section of the AT, from Tricorner Knob to Davenport Gap, we were uncomfortable with the option.

Retracing our steps to Newfound Gap would mean hiking about 15.4 miles over terrain we were familiar with. We knew the hike would be difficult, with over 4,100 feet in ascent and 5,000 feet in descent, steep uphill and downhill sections, and almost no flat trail. We had the comfort of knowing the car would be there waiting for us when we arrived, and if for some reason we had an issue, we could always stop at the Icewater Spring shelter, which was only three miles from the vehicle.

There were more variables we had control over if we

backtracked to Newfound Gap, so the decision was clear, we needed to turn around and retrace our steps to the car.

Based on our hiking pace the previous two days and adding in the soreness and exhaustion we had developed, we estimated we could maintain a pace of twenty to thirty minutes per mile. This meant the hike would take between six and eight hours, which included a break for lunch. We didn't know what time the bad weather was forecasted to arrive, and we didn't want to risk driving in a snowstorm, so we decided to set our alarm for 5:00 A.M. and to be on the trail by 5:30.

***

Using our headlamps to illuminate the trail, our pace that morning was great. We were full of energy and adrenaline, primarily from our motivation to avoid the bad weather. The hike was physically tough, but the thought of a hot meal that night, and a real bed in a climate-controlled room, made the pain easier to overcome.

Reaching Charlie's Bunion around 11:00 A.M. was a mental relief, knowing we were only four miles from the car with just one climb left to tackle. The view from the Bunion was almost non-existent with heavy fog limiting our visibility to a few hundred feet.

Resting a good twenty to thirty minutes while we ate an early lunch, we took notice that we had not seen a single person all day. Then, as soon as we threw our packs on for the final leg of the hike, snow started falling. We were only 1.5 hours from the car, so we knew we could get off the trail before any serious accumulation occurred. In a sense, it was a relief to see the snow, as it validated our decision to wake up early and hike back to the car.

It was snowing lightly when we arrived back to the car

around 1:00 P.M. Checking the weather forecast again out of curiosity, we were amazed to see over a foot of snow forecasted for the next twenty-four hours and temperatures in the single digits.

The road to Newfound Gap, Hwy 441, was closed to all traffic at 2:45 P.M., less than two hours after we exited the trail. If we had continued as planned - which we would have if not for the reports from other hikers - we would have been stranded until Monday in all likelihood. There were many reports over the next few days of park rangers riding snow machines to rescue hikers from shelters throughout the park.

Looking back at the progression of the weather forecast, the initial Winter Storm Warning was issued Thursday afternoon around the time we arrived at Tricorner Knob. It stated:

...SNOWFALL ACCUMULATIONS BETWEEN 4 AND 8 INCHES ARE EXPECTED FOR MOST LOCATIONS ABOVE 2500 FEET. LOCALLY HIGHER AMOUNTS UP TO A FOOT OR MORE WILL BE POSSIBLE ACROSS THE HIGHEST PEAKS ABOVE 5000 FEET.

By Saturday, the National Weather Service revised its warning to say:

...SNOWFALL ACCUMULATIONS BETWEEN 6 T0 12 INCHES ARE EXPECTED FOR MOST LOCATIONS ABOVE 2500 FEET. LOCALLY HIGHER AMOUNTS UP TO 18 INCHES OR MORE WILL BE POSSIBLE ACROSS THE HIGHEST PEAKS ABOVE 5000 FEET.

It was hard to believe the dramatic change in forecasts. We had checked the forecast before the trip and again on Thursday morning at the Icewater Spring shelter, but it still was not enough to prepare for the situation. Wednesday afternoon, there was only a slight chance for an inch or two of snow occurring Friday night and into Saturday. But in the end, the official snow accumulation came in at twenty-two inches, with a low temperature of nine degrees F.

***

While the situation would have been very unpleasant had we continued the trip as planned, potentially being forced to spend an extra two to three nights in a shelter, we do not believe it would have been life threatening. We had shelter, we had water, and we had extra food. We had warm clothes, and besides Josh only having a twenty-degree sleeping bag, he would have survived by wearing extra clothes while in his bag. I also had my personal satellite distress beacon and knew that at any time I could press one button and have a search and rescue team dispatched to come get us (if the storm conditions allowed it).

The trip highlighted the need to pack extra supplies in case we are forced to stay longer than expected, and the importance of letting someone know our exact plans; including a plan if someone does not hear from us by a certain time. We were lucky to receive an updated forecast Thursday afternoon, but I often think about what may have happened if we had not. With this thought in the back of my mind, I now plan all future trips with the mindset that a similar event may occur.

WIND AND RAIN

In the fall of 2015, Josh and I decided to take another trip on the AT in North Carolina. Like the previous year, Josh would start before me on a Saturday, and I would meet him later in the week. Josh would start at Davenport Gap (where we had planned to finish our hike the previous year) and over the course of three days, he would hike approximately thirty-four miles to Hot Springs, NC where I would meet him Tuesday morning. Our plan was then to hike around forty-five miles from Hot Springs to Interstate 26 over a four-day period.

We emailed our itinerary to our emergency contacts as shown below:

AT Trip 2015 - Davenport Gap to Sam's Gap – 80miles Saturday October 24th – Friday October 30th

Sat Oct 24th- Davenport Gap I-40 to Ground Hog Creek Shelter

Sun Oct 25th- Ground Hog to Walnut Mountain Shelter

Mon Oct 26th- Walnut Mountain to Hot Springs NC (Iron Horse Hotel Hot Springs)

Tue Oct 27th- Hot Springs to Spring Mountain Shelter (meet Colby 10:00am)

Wed Oct 28th- Spring Mountain to Jerry Cabin Shelter

Thu Oct 29th- Jerry Cabin to Big Flat Camp

Fri Oct 30th- Big Flat to Sam's Gap I-26 (AT parking Sam's Gap: 4460 Flag Pond Rd, Mars Hill NC/TN. Mandie picking us up Friday morning at Sam's Gap 11:00am)

Even though shelters were available along the trail, we packed our tents with the intent of using them at or near the shelters, giving us a little more privacy from other hikers and pesky mice. The plan for day one was pretty solid: we'd hike a steady uphill 2,100-foot climb over eleven miles to the Spring Mountain shelter. The following days we had goals set on where to camp but would just play it by ear each day on whether to hike a little farther or less than planned; as long as we made it to Interstate 26 by 11:00 A.M. Friday, we would be fine.

Monday morning, with Josh already on the trail, we exchanged a couple emails:

Josh:
In Hot Springs, made crazy good time, did 16miles sat and 18 miles sunday. walked in to Hot Springs Sunday night at 5:00pm. pretty sore so using today(monday) as a zero day/rest day. This town has zero cell serv for att and verizon. only US celluar evidently. and wifi is super spotty so com's a no go. I'll meet you tomorrow morning in front of or near the iron horse... trail was pretty good all things considered. See you tuesday morning. don't forget my food/gear!

My Response:
Geeze that's a lot of hiking. I should be there around 930 tomorrow morning. Got my rain pants, looks like a complete washout all day tomorrow, and just a few hours of rain in the late afternoon Wednesday.

As noted in the email Monday, there was already heavy rain in the forecast for Tuesday. The National Weather Service issued the following High Wind Watch soon after I composed that email:

254 PM EDT MON OCT 26 2015
...HIGH WIND WATCH IN EFFECT FROM TUESDAY EVENING THROUGH WEDNESDAY MORNING...
* HAZARDS...DAMAGING WINDS POSSIBLE.
* TIMING...TUESDAY EVENING INTO WEDNESDAY MORNING.
* WINDS...SOUTHEAST 30 TO 40 MPH WITH GUSTS OF 60 TO 65 MPH POSSIBLE.
* IMPACTS...DUE TO EXPECTED RAINFALL AND THESE HIGH WINDS...NUMEROUS TREES AND POWERLINES MAY FALL LEADING TO SCATTERED POWER OUTAGES.

Multiple weather issues now had to be considered. High winds that would create falling tree hazards, cold temperatures in the forties, and heavy rain were now expected. Rain, cold, and high winds do not mix well for outdoor activities.

***

I arrived in Hot Springs Tuesday morning around 9:00 A.M. with a stomach that did not feel well. I had been up the previous night with an upset stomach, so my energy level was low; and I knew I was not fully hydrated. But with rain forecasted to begin late morning, and the wind to pick up substantially in the afternoon, I was motivated to get on the trail and to the shelter as quickly as possible.

The trail initially followed the banks of the French

Broad River and then steeply climbed 1,200 feet over the next two miles. Rain began to fall almost immediately after we started. I had my rain cover over my pack, my North Face Gore-Tex rain jacket and pants on, and had my heavy-duty Gore-Tex hiking boots on, so I was confident my body and gear would stay dry. But carrying a thirty-five-pound pack uphill, while wearing a rain jacket and rain pants, caused me to generate a lot of body heat.

I rolled up my jacket sleeves and opened the armpit air vents to cool off. As much as I wanted to remove my jacket, I knew I'd never get my clothes dry again once they were wet, creating a potentially dangerous situation that could lead to hypothermia.

The rain gear quickly became a burden. We were both sweating a lot, even though it was a cool forty-five degrees. Josh's water was tucked away under his pack's rain cover, making it difficult to grab without either taking the pack off or having me grab it for him. This led to him not drinking enough water during the hike, but luckily he was well hydrated from the previous day. I had a CamelBak bladder in my pack, with a long tube that provided me access to water at any time while we hiked; but starting off the hike dehydrated that morning put me way behind in the hydration game.

I started the hike with a single energy bar in my jacket pocket for quick access, but the rest of my food was zipped up in the outer pouch of my pack. Typically, Josh and I would unzip each other's packs to get any requested food or snacks out; or we would take our packs off and quickly grab what we needed. With the rain covers on, accessing food was no longer a quick and easy task; therefore we didn't eat our trail snacks like we normally would.

With the rain and wind picking up, getting to the

shelter was our top priority. We were sweating a lot, so anytime we stopped to rest, we would get cold quickly from the inactivity. Cutting our rest stops short, we would start hiking again just to warm up.

The ground was soaking wet and the rain fell steadily, so we rarely sat down out of fear of us and our gear getting wet. Over the entire eleven-mile hike, our longest rest stop was sitting down with our packs on for five minutes.

By the time we were a mile from the shelter, I was completely exhausted. I had eaten almost no food, was still dehydrated, my stomach was still not feeling well, and we had only sat down once. I was not sure I had the energy to continue, and my body was telling me to stop. My legs didn't want to move, no thanks to the heavy hiking boots I was wearing.

Josh noticed how much I was struggling and acted quickly. If the weather was decent, we would have sat down and rested for a while, and if needed, pitched the tents where we were. But it just was not safe to do so.

Josh's pack weighed a little less than mine, so we switched packs and he pushed on ahead to the shelter, leaving me behind to continue at a turtle's pace. The thoughts going through my head included how could I safely stop and make a shelter where I was, and what would I do if Josh did not make it back. The rain kept falling and the wind had increased to at least thirty-five to forty miles-per-hour. I knew there were not any safe options but to continue pressing forward.

It felt like an eternity before I saw Josh coming up the trail towards me. He had dropped my gear at the shelter and came back to carry his pack (the pack I was now carrying) the rest of the way to the shelter. What a difference that made for me. About ten more minutes of hiking and we were at the shelter, Spring Mountain.

***

The Spring Mountain shelter was very small, with a maximum capacity of five people. It was built in the early 1930's and is one of the oldest shelters on the AT. While the history and character of the shelter was great, I was really hoping for a shelter like those in GSMNP; and if not for the high wind and rain, we would have set up our tents instead due to the small size and lack of personal space in the shelter.

Two other men were in the shelter when we arrived: southbound thru-hikers hiking together for the past three months. They had hung their tent across the front of the shelter to create a wind and rain barrier, keeping us dry and relatively warm inside.

Not much happened that night besides being stuck in a confined space with a couple of strangers. We exchanged a few stories, talked about how miserable we all were, cooked our dinners, and went to bed.

The next morning the weather had cleared up nicely. There was still a little wind and fog, but the rain had stopped. We refilled our water from a natural spring nearby, and then continued our hike northward.

While I was hiking in the lead, I noticed a large animal coming towards us on the trail. At first, I thought it was a coyote. Having seen many coyotes while hunting, I quickly realized it was much larger and resembled the very rare red wolf found in North Carolina. I stopped and called out to make him aware of our presence, and as soon as he saw me, he took off quickly into the thick brush.

Reaching a paved road crossing after about four miles of hiking, Josh wanted to take an extended break; he was developing hip pain from all the downhill hiking that morning. Our map indicated another natural spring near the road crossing we were at, however, even after the previous night's rain, the spring was completely dry.

This was a major issue. In an effort to reduce pack weight, we only refilled enough water at the shelter to get us to this point. We were both extremely low on water, and our trail guide indicated the next water source was another five miles ahead; which was at the next shelter we were hiking to.

With our low water supply, Josh's hip pain, and me still not at 100%, we sat down and discussed what to do. This was the last paved road for the next twenty-two miles, and we had another thirty miles and 2.5 days of hiking to reach our exit.

After much deliberation, we decided to abandon our hike completely and head back to Hot Springs; though we weren't exactly sure how to do that.

Our first thought was to call a shuttle service in Hot Springs to pick us up, however, that quickly became a non-option as we had no cell service. So, we pulled out the map to see if the trail would offer our most direct route back or if any Forest Service roads were around that could get us back quicker. We also looked at how long it would take hiking the paved roads to get back. Unfortunately, every option required at least fifteen miles of hiking.

We decided on a new tactic, something neither of us had ever done and had been told to never do, even though it is fairly common among AT thru-hikers: we put our thumbs out with every car that drove by and attempted to hitchhike. [Well, not every car, some looked a little sketchy and we did not feel like being kidnapped.]

Our first ride was in an old station wagon driven by a young man. He took us to an intersection a few miles up the road and dropped us off. Our next ride was from a lady in a Ford Ranger pickup, who took us a good way back towards Hot Springs but had to drop us off at another intersection as well. Lastly, a man in an old Toyota Land Cruiser picked us up and drove us into Hot Springs.

***

Dinner that night in Hot Springs was fantastic, much better than the freeze-dried meal I had planned to eat. We ate at the Spring Creek Tavern on a deck overlooking a large creek. We drank a couple beers, ate a lot of food, and then about halfway through our dinner, the guys we had spent the previous night with at the shelter walked over. We all hung out for a while, then Josh and I went back to the Iron Horse hotel where we both slept great on warm and comfortable beds.

The next day we drove to Max Patch mountain on the Tennessee/North Carolina border. The AT passes directly over top of the bald mountain summit and provides amazing 360-degree views. Josh hiked this section a few days earlier, and he suggested we backpack to a flat spot and camp there for our final night. When we started the hike, clouds and fog obstructed our view, but once we arrived at our campsite, calm blue skies appeared and made for a perfect afternoon and a beautiful sunset.

Our night spent on Max Patch was not part of the plan. We should have been more than halfway to our exit point on the original trek; yet we were both content sitting on the mountain admiring the world around us. I pulled out my camera and started taking pictures; one of the photos was of Josh overlooking the mountains during sunset, which ended up becoming the cover photo of this book.

This was on a Thursday night in the fall of 2015, and there was not a single other person to be seen. Unfortunately, some local Asheville guides started highly publicizing the area soon after, and now it is a place to avoid due to the heavy crowds (the U.S. Forest Service implemented new land-use policies for the area in July 2021). A one-lane Forest Service road leads to the mountain, and I have been stuck on this road for over an hour due to the volume of cars. The parking lot at the trailhead can occupy about ten cars, a lot less than the seventy-five to one-hundred cars that line the road at any given time on a typical weekend.

***

Almost nothing about this trip went as planned. Being flexible and stepping outside of my comfort zone were both tested. I came to the realization that most backpacking trips I had taken did not go as planned, and the best practice is to be mentally prepared for any unplanned event.

At the time we made the decision to abandon our hike, it felt like we were quitters and losers, that we would be embarrassed to even tell anyone what we did. But accepting the fact that there were things outside of our control, such as the weather and dry water source, and combining those factors with the physical ailments we were both experiencing, we are now proud of the decision we made to abandon the original hike.

I think too many people are focused on achieving a goal, fearing failure or appearing weak. The end goal for me is to enjoy the moment and return home safely, which is exactly what we did.

When it comes to actionable lessons learned, there were a few. First, I will never wear heavy duty hiking boots again on a well-worn trail. The additional weight of these boots and the reduced mobility was a major drag, costing me a lot of energy. There is an adage that for every pound on your feet equals five pounds on your back. From now on, I wear lightweight shoes on all my backpacking trips, such as La Sportiva approach shoes or North Face hiking shoes.

Second, I learned about gear that I do not need. For example, it is not necessary to pack more than one flashlight, as it is too redundant and adds too much weight. This is especially true when hiking with someone that has a flashlight as well.

Third, when hiking in the rain, wear as few layers as possible under your rain gear, as it is very difficult to shed layers in the rain; and wearing rain gear will trap heat excessively. Also, put as many snacks as possible in your pockets, since getting into your pack will be difficult with the rain cover on. And lastly, put essential gear such as a sleeping bag and tent into a drybag.

The author setting up camp at Max Patch

Josh in the Icewater Spring shelter

Josh hiking at Charlie's Bunion

6 - THE INHOSPITABLE WEST

TRIP PLANNING

It was June 2015 when I boarded a plane with my friends Josh and Chris (not to be confused with my brother Christopher). This was Josh and Chris's first time to Utah, and excluding a previous work trip, was my first time as well. We had taken the entire week off work and had an ambitious plan for hiking, backpacking, and sightseeing across the entire state.

Our preparation began in late 2014 when Josh and I came up with the trip idea while hiking the AT in GSMNP. My day-hiking experience in Colorado, California, and Idaho was the closest any of us had come to backpacking in the Western environment, so we knew the trip would be an exploration for all of us.

Josh and I had the benefit of completing a multi-night backpacking trip together prior to the trip, so we knew each other's strengths and weaknesses. Chris had little backpacking and wilderness experience, but he enjoyed camping and adventure. I had camped with him a couple of times prior to this trip, including an overnight kayaking trip in the Okefenokee and a trip to Cumberland Island.

Josh and I took the lead on researching backpacking trails and other areas to visit. We purchased and studied topo maps of all the national parks in Utah, and read backpacking and hiking forums on the internet. After months of research, we choose two national parks to plan our trip around: Canyonlands and Zion.

Backpacking was on our itinerary for both national parks. The first trek would be in the Needles District of Canyonlands National Park. We planned to follow the Salt Creek trail from Cathedral Butte to Squaw Flat. Over a four-day period, we would be required to hike a total of 27.5 miles over strenuous terrain.

The second hike would be in Zion National Park. We planned to complete The Narrows from the top-down, meaning we would need to hike sixteen miles over two days from Chamberlain's Ranch to the Temple of Sinawava. The trail environment in Zion looked very different than Canyonlands. We'd be hiking directly in a river and out of the sun for the majority of the Zion trek, versus the open desert sand and plateaus of Canyonlands.

Our ambitious plan would expose us to different landscapes and environments, which complicated our packing as each hike required different gear.

Attempting almost fifty miles of backpacking in the June desert heat and knowing we'd be at a much higher altitude than in Georgia, we were motivated to begin a workout regimen to get into proper physical shape. Josh and I ran twice weekly on cross country trails for a few months leading up to the trip, and Chris ran daily on a treadmill.

Both backpacking treks required permits, which we secured about four months before the trip. Knowing our routes were confirmed, we were able to begin detailed trip planning.

Logistically, we needed to secure transportation for both backpacking treks, as both were one-way hikes. We contacted shuttle services in Moab for the Canyonlands portion and in Springdale for the Zion portion, and booked two shuttles; even after hearing their exorbitant fees.

I studied topo maps, aerial imagery, and read trip reports from others who had completed the same hikes. Having spent hours researching potential water sources on the Salt Creek trail, the availability of water on the Canyonlands hike became the overarching concern and biggest unknown; the consequences of running out of water in the desert would be deadly. The trip was in early June, so the temperature would most likely be in the nineties or even hundreds, and knowing the trail had very little shade, a high-water intake would be essential.

I decided to call the ranger station in Canyonlands to speak with a park ranger, and asked about creeks and springs that I had either seen on the map or read about online. The ranger told me there "should" be a few water sources, but to still carry as much water as possible, as nothing was guaranteed. After that conversation, a few weeks before the trip, I sent out an email to Josh and Chris:

Water sources are good right now, but they expect when we are there that a lot will be dried up and we will have long sections without water, so bring a lot of containers.

Josh responded:

Water might be an issue but it's not like we can really afford not [to] carry a lot.

According to NPS website they recommend drinking at least one gallon of water a day

One large (32oz) Nalgene bottle filled up weighs about 2 pounds so carrying a lot of water really adds up in extra weight. Carrying a gallon of water is 8 extra pounds but prob worth it for the first day, two bottles plus a camel back should come close to 1 gallon.

I'm also bringing my water filter bottle and filling that and drinking from it whenever I come across a stream/creek crossing.

Basically I'm just going to refill whatever chance I get
–Josh

Our Canyonlands permit was sent over via email and contained a copy of the Canyonlands Backcountry Information Guide. Some of the ominous warnings in the guide included:

Heat, intense sunlight, low humidity, and high elevation require people to adapt to harsh desert conditions. Carry and drink at least one gallon of water each day; more if involved in strenuous activities. Avoid overexposure to intense sun. During hotter times of the year, save strenuous activity for mornings or evenings.

Storms and flash floods can hit suddenly and without warning. During a lightning storm avoid lone trees, cliff edges and high ridges. Return to your vehicle if possible. Crouch low to the ground. Flash floods can occur without warning. Never camp in a dry wash or try to cross a wash during flood conditions.

Stay with companions in the backcountry; separation can mean getting lost. Carry a map and compass and know how to use them. Do not count on a cellular phone to summon help, as cellular service will not reach into many areas of the canyon country. If you become lost, stay where you are and wait for rescue. Wandering will endanger your life and make finding you difficult.

Treat all water found in the backcountry. Using a filter, iodine tablets or boiling water for up to five minutes are the most efficient ways of eliminating waterborne bacteria.

Knowing cell phone service would be non-existent, I downloaded both aerial imagery and topo maps onto my phone. Even without cell service, GPS can still work on a smartphone, and since the maps and imagery were downloaded, my phone would be able to provide reliable navigation so long as I could keep it charged. Expecting four days without access to electricity, I packed a small, portable, solar powered cell phone charger; and in an effort to preserve battery life, I planned to keep my phone turned off except while checking our location or taking photos.

In regard to our gear, Josh and I already owned most of the items needed. Chris, on the other hand, did not have much. With our guidance, Chris went out and bought a lightweight backpacking tent, sleeping bag, sleeping pad, backpack, camping stove, water bladder, and water filter.

One item we all had to purchase was specialized shoes. The Narrows hike would require hiking directly in the river for over ten miles, meaning good water shoes and neoprene socks were necessary. Searching online for 'canyoneering shoes' provided us with a lot of resources to pick out the perfect pair, which I ended up purchasing a pair of Merrells.

Traveling 2,000 miles from Georgia to Utah meant we

would need to fly. Our packs were large and full of camping gear, so we purchased some Osprey pack carriers, or Airporter bags, to add some protection from the airline baggage handlers. We could not pack all the items we needed due to airline regulations, so we had to wait until we arrived in Utah to purchase gear such as lighters and camp fuel; and in order to stay under the fifty-pound bag limit with the airline, we decided to purchase our food after we arrived as well.

The most difficult piece of gear I had to pack was a bear vault. Our hike in Canyonlands had strict requirements regarding food storage, and the only approved method of storage was to use a bear vault. One vault was required per permit, and I was the one who would pack and carry it. The circular shaped vault was made of heavy-duty plastic and was about nine inches high by nine inches in diameter. It was bulky and heavy, both things to avoid when selecting backpacking gear, but we had no other choice.

We double and triple checked all our gear, and provided our emergency contacts with a detailed itinerary, then departed Atlanta before sunrise Saturday morning and flew to Salt Lake City.

CANYONLANDS NATIONAL PARK

After a quick stop at Cabela's to pick up some gear, we then drove four hours from Salt Lake City to Moab. The weather was hit or miss the entire drive, with sporadic storms and downpours, followed by clear skies and bright sunshine. These storms were not typical for the desert in early June (monsoon season is typically mid-July through mid-September), and many severe thunderstorm and flash flood warnings were issued across the state.

Arriving in Moab that evening, we checked into our hotel, grabbed a bite to eat, then spent the remainder of the evening getting our packs ready for the four-day hike in Canyonlands.

Chris was taking items out of his bag when Josh and I noticed a lot of his gear was still in its original packaging, including his tent, water bladder, and water filter. Josh and I looked at each other with the same thought of 'dude, seriously, you didn't think to test out your gear before going on a four-day trip in the desert.' Needless to say, Chris spent the next couple hours learning about his new gear, including at least thirty minutes figuring out how to use the water filter.

The following morning, we woke up early and drove seventy-five miles to the Needles District of Canyonlands National Park. Arriving at the visitor center, we checked-in at the wilderness desk as mandated by our permit.

The rangers made sure we had the required gear, including a bear vault, compass, map, flashlight, and water. They made us aware of flash flooding that occurred the previous night in the park and warned us to be careful when around any creeks, as more rain was forecasted over the coming days.

One of the rangers recently completed the hike we were attempting, and she provided us a little comfort when she said most water sources were reliable.

The rangers asked how we planned to get to our starting point, Cathedral Butte, as it was many miles down a dirt road with hazardous creek crossings; some of which may be washed out from the previous day's rain. Letting them know we had a shuttle coming, they assured us our shuttle driver would be experienced and prepared for any road hazards.

At 9:00 A.M. we met our shuttle driver. He was an old

hippie, driving a non-lifted, non-four-wheel-drive, 20+ year old VW van. If the rangers were correct in their assessment of the dirt road, there was no way this vehicle would make it. Josh looked at Chris and me, and said "You've got to be kidding me, is this a joke."

The company required prepayment, which was paid via $300 check weeks before the trip, so there was no backing out now. I even spoke with the owner of the company the night before, which she ensured me they had a lifted four-wheel-drive vehicle for us since the road would most likely have some issues. Raising our concerns with the driver, he responded in a high-on-life hippie way, "No man it's going to be all good, this thing has over a million miles on it, it can go anywhere."

With no other option but to trust his judgement, we skeptically loaded our gear in the van and hit the road. The first ten to fifteen minutes of the shuttle ride was back down the paved road that we had driven in on, then we turned onto a dirt road. Hippie guy had not stopped talking about how amazing his van was and continued to project confidence that we would make it to our destination.

No sooner had we started down the dirt road, the shuttle driver stopped just short of a large creek crossing. The water was flowing rapidly, and the banks had caved in. For the first time hippie guy finally stopped talking. He stepped out of the van, walked around for a minute, and hopped back into the driver's seat. He then quickly threw the van into reverse and nonchalantly says "Looks like we can't go any farther."

"What!? We just asked you a few minutes ago and you said the road would be fine, and not to worry!"

We were not happy; this was our only option to get to the trailhead, we already paid the company, and we already had our permits secured for the hike.

A very arrogant and condescending conversation took place between us and the driver during the fifteen-minute drive back to the park. We suspected he knew the road was impassable for the ill-equipped van, as he drove right by the dirt road earlier when he came to get us that morning.

A few weeks later, we ended up receiving a mere $50 refund out of the $300 we paid, which was not nearly enough. I know one thing for sure is that we will never use nor recommend that shuttle service again.

Back at the visitor center feeling angry and defeated, we went inside to talk to the rangers about our options. I couldn't believe our trip had literally just started and we already had to change our plans drastically.

Our original permit had us camping at the Upper Salt 3 campsite, Upper Salt 4 campsite, and then open camping in the Salt/Horse zone. Since we were now forced to start and end our hike from the same location, there was no possible way to follow the same itinerary. The rangers helped us rework our plan, and suggested we hike the same trail as before as an out and back trip, rather than attempting the entire distance.

They issued us a new permit that had us starting at Squaw Flat (where we originally planned to end our hike) and then open camp in the Salt/Horse zone for all three nights. We were now looking to hike around seven miles the first day, another six miles the second day, then turn around and hike back seven to eight miles the third day, and finish with about seven miles the fourth and final day. To our satisfaction, the new plan provided us with roughly the same amount of backpacking as the original, about twenty-six to twenty-seven miles.

***

Under partly cloudy skies with temperatures in the eighties, we began our hike on an open, flat, and well-marked trail. Our fast pace was not hindered until we reached a steep slick rock climb a couple miles into the hike. Using our hands to help us up, we reached the top of the climb and had our first grand view of the park.

The next few miles were filled with steep climbs and descents in and out of the canyon. The route finding was difficult in some sections, but by following cairns (stacked rocks to indicate the trail) we managed to stay on course.

With the sun bearing down, we took frequent breaks anywhere we could find shade, and around mile four, we sat down underneath a small overhang. We were on slickrock which was angled about thirty degrees downhill and straight into a canyon. We removed our packs, sat down, and pulled out some snacks.

Chris had his small cooking fuel canister towards the top of his pack and needed to remove it to access his snacks. He grabbed the canister and placed it on the ground, where it immediately began rolling down the slickrock towards the canyon.

I instinctively reached out when it started rolling, but did not even bother to chase it, knowing it was gone. It disappeared off the edge and fell deep into the canyon a few seconds later. We walked to the edge and looked for a route down, but the sheer drop was at least seventy-five feet. As much as we hated leaving trash in the wilderness, we did not have a choice.

If Chris were hiking the trail alone, losing his one and only fuel canister would have been a serious determent, resulting in either needing to abandon the hike entirely, or having to build a fire each night to cook over. Thankfully, Josh and I both had small fuel canisters with us that we knew would provide enough fuel for everyone, so we continued on with the hike.

Instead of rappelling sections, the Park Service placed two permanent ladders on the trail, one of which was in a very narrow slot, descending about fifteen to twenty feet, and with a very difficult dismount. Josh was the first to descend the ladder. About halfway down, his progress stopped, and he let out a few yells, saying "I'm stuck!" and "Get me out of here!".

Chris and I could not see what was happening and did not know how to help beside telling him to just keep trying. A few moments later, he reached the bottom. According to Josh, his pack was too wide and became wedged in the narrow slot. After jumping up and down on the ladder a few times, he broke loose, but also tore a hole in the rain jacket strapped on the side of his pack.

After the precarious ladder descent, we passed through the Peekaboo campsite and entered the Salt/Horse zone around mile five, meaning we could begin our search for a place to camp; though we decided to hike on for another hour or so.

The trail began to follow Salt Creek, which was nothing more than a dried-up creek bed. Without a clearly defined trail in many places, we followed the creek bed as indicated on our map. Our pace slowed significantly, not because of any steep climbs or descents, but rather from hiking through the deep and soft sand that made up the canyon floor.

Out of nowhere, thunder began to echo through the canyon walls, and looking towards the sky, the sun had disappeared. Dark, ominous clouds filled the horizon, prompting us to don our rain gear. The storm was moving slowly from west to east, so I suggested we hold our current position to the north.

Josh suggested otherwise and wanted to move forward to find a decent camping spot, meaning we would hike directly towards the storm. Following Josh's lead, we continued down the trail in a light rain, and then a half-mile later, came across the perfect campsite.

The weather cleared up as soon as we arrived, and we unpacked our gear and set up camp under the bright sun. Josh and I had our tents erected and gear unpacked quickly, then explored the surrounding area; while Chris spent an hour struggling to set up his tent for the first time. Finding a very small creek a few hundred feet away, we filled up our containers with what turned out to be the only flowing water we would encounter on the trek.

Dinner that evening consisted of freeze-dried meals for all of us. I had a chicken and rice Mountain House meal, which is something I had many times before. Purposely choosing a familiar meal, I knew how it would taste and that it would not cause any stomach distress. I have tried many varieties of freeze-dried meals, and the chicken and rice had always tasted great and sat well on my stomach.

Josh brought a three-bean chili freeze-dried meal, a dish he had never tried before. While he claims it tasted great, it did not sit well on his stomach, and ended up putting a damper on his energy level over the next twenty-four hours. Needless to say, I do not think he will ever purchase that variety again.

Our camp for night #1

Hiking on day #1

***

Shortly after sunrise the following morning, we packed up our gear and continued south on an obvious trail next to the creek. Our goal was to reach the next campsite before the afternoon heat set-in.

The trail quickly became difficult to follow, with

multiple intersections and a lot of tall underbrush. Josh was in the lead, directly in front of me, when suddenly his body disappeared while he let out a yell.

We were walking in such high grass that he could not see the three-foot bank in front of him, which he stepped off and into a small pool of water about knee deep. Josh was shaken, but uninjured, and I helped him back up the embankment. With the trail rapidly becoming difficult to follow, we decided to pause for a moment to check our bearing.

Pulling out my cell phone, I powered it on and opened the aerial imagery. Our GPS location appeared on the image, which created immediate concern. The trail track (a series of GPS waypoints) I had downloaded was a long distance away from our current location, and I had no idea how we got so far off course.

When I informed Josh and Chris that we had hiked deep into a side canyon putting us way off course, they argued that it was not possible; that either the GPS or trail track was incorrect. I was confident in the trail track I had downloaded, and knew the GPS could not be that far off, but I knew it was best to use all the tools available to determine our location accurately.

I pulled out the hard copy topo map and determined our location by correlating the UTM coordinates from my phone with the UTM grid on the map. Exactly like the aerial imagery, our location on the hard copy map indicated we were off course; about a mile deep into a side canyon.

Dispirited, we hiked the twenty minutes back to our campsite wondering where and how we screwed up. Back at the campsite, having already wasted an hour of hiking, I checked our location again using my GPS. We were still off course, but this time only by a few hundred yards.

We soon realized our mistake: while searching for a campsite the day before, we ended up walking off the main trail; the trail we took was simply a spur to access the campsite.

This did not explain the existence of the obvious path we wrongly followed that morning. If we were unable to acquire our GPS coordinates, I do not believe we would have turned around. Without the GPS, this wrong turn could have been a huge detriment. The side canyon continued for another few miles, and we would have probably made it to the end before turning around, effectively losing an entire day of progress.

Knowing we were back on track, we continued south on the correct trail with the goal of reaching a highly regarded campsite. Even with our hour-long delay, we arrived at the site shortly before noon.

A giant cottonwood tree was the centerpiece of the site, nestled near a portion of Salt Creek containing large pools of water. Many large petroglyphs and granaries located high up on the canyon walls were visible from the site, providing a sense of stepping back in time. I imagined this was exactly the conditions ancient civilizations endured, and I wondered how they survived in such an arid environment with little wildlife.

The remoteness of our location was apparent. Over twenty-four hours and thirteen miles of desert had passed since we began our hike, and we had only seen one other set of backpackers. Aside from my emergency satellite beacon, contact with the outside world was not possible. We were over twenty miles from cell service and a full day's hike to the closest road.

There were no worries from the outside world and no other people to bother us, it was truly just us; we were secluded, exhausted, and content in the inhospitable desert.

We made camp under the cottonwood tree, and then Josh and I explored the surrounding canyon walls while Chris took a nap. Then, with Chris refreshed, we put on our daypacks for a three-mile round trip hike to Angel Arch.

The arch, resembling the shape of an angel, is one of the most remote arches in the park, accessible only by a twenty-six-mile round trip hike. Most arches of that stature are surrounded by tourists on a daily basis, but given the remote location, we enjoyed the arch completely to ourselves.

Back at camp, I downed a few Ibuprofen with my dinner and then crawled into my sleeping bag around 9:00 P.M. Tired from two days of hiking, and with the overnight lows dropping into the fifties, we all slept great that night.

Camp setup for night #2
***

Expecting temperatures nearing one-hundred degrees on our third day, we wasted no time the following morning loading up our gear and hitting the trail with hopes to reach our next campsite before noon.

Josh led the way with a fast and determined pace, retracing our steps towards the car. With very few rest stops, the steady pace over seven miles brought us to the Salt/Horse zone boundary in just a few hours.

I focused on finding an area to set up camp since we had no plans to hike any farther that day; Josh focused on finding water, since he was completely out; and Chris was slowly, yet steadily, bringing up the rear.

Josh found a small pool of stagnant and warm water a few yards off the trail. With him being out of water, and Chris and I running low, we refilled half of our containers - only half because the water looked like a breeding ground for bacteria, and we expected another water source a little farther up the trail near the Peekaboo area.

Reaching Peekaboo fifteen minutes later, a little farther than we had intended to hike that day, Chris and I were ready to quit and make camp. We were exhausted, hungry, and thirsty, so we laid down on a couple of large, shaded rocks and rested.

While resting, Josh began to talk about pushing on and finishing the hike to the car that day, rather than making camp and hiking out the next day as planned. The temperature was pushing one-hundred degrees, and I did not want to walk anymore. Chris did not say much, and he appeared very exhausted, having visually sweated a lot. I suggested we rest a little longer, then bring it up again for discussion.

Not long after, Chris commented that his urine was very dark; a general indication that he was dehydrated. Josh, having a single packet of electrolyte mix left, gave it to Chris to mix with his water. Soon after chugging the liter of electrolyte mixed water, Chris had to pee again; this time having completely clear urine. At the time, we all thought this was a good sign, as we had been taught that clear urine means you are hydrated.

Around the same time, we noticed a lot of water on the ground, and quickly realized Chris's water bladder was leaking from its mouthpiece. Chris had drunk all the water from his Nalgene, and since the rest of his water was stored in the bladder, he was now left with less than half a liter of water after stopping the leak.

Between the three of us, we had about three liters of water left. This was not of any concern if we were staying put the rest of the day, but Josh really wanted to push on to the car. Eventually, yet reluctantly, Chris and I agreed to push on and hike the last five miles; even with our low water supply and in the high afternoon heat. Why did we make this decision? In hindsight it makes no sense, but the dehydration and extreme heat we were experiencing probably hindered our reasoning abilities.

Only a half mile past Peekaboo was the narrow slot with the tall ladder, which marked the beginning of a steep and shadeless slickrock climb to the top of the canyon. Quickly reaching the top of the canyon with Josh's steady pace, and taking notice of a narrow sliver of shade, Chris asked if we could take a break. He said he was nauseated, dizzy, overheated, and generally felt unwell.

We immediately sat him down in the shade and told him we could rest there for as long as he needed. I dampened my bandana with water and gave it to him to wrap around his neck.

Believing he was suffering from heat exhaustion, the decision was made to stay put in the shade while he cooled off; and then when he was able, we would hike back down to Peekaboo and camp for the night. There was no way Chris was in any kind of condition to hike four more miles, and I was mad at myself for attempting this unplanned push to the car.

Chris was the first to run out of water, happening only a few minutes after we stopped to rest. Not long after, Josh and I were down to a half liter between us. Chris's condition was not improving, but thankfully it wasn't getting any worse.

Josh and I discussed having one of us descend into the canyon to find water, but before we made a decision, the wind suddenly picked up. We walked out onto the slickrock to get a better view of the sky, where we saw very dark and fast-moving clouds heading our way. Knowing we were exposed at the top of the canyon, and not wanting to be stuck there during a thunderstorm, we decided to take advantage of the cool wind and cloud cover to hike back down to Peekaboo.

Placing a lot of Chris's gear into my pack, Josh then carried both his own and Chris's pack, one on each shoulder. Walking directly behind Chris, I kept one hand on the back of his shirt to make sure he did not lose his footing on the steep descent down to the canyon floor. Of most concern was the narrow and long ladder, as a fall off the ladder would have resulted in a serious injury. We made it down slowly and safely and arrived back to the Peekaboo camp area before any rain or lightning appeared.

All Chris wanted to do was lie down and rest. The wind had picked up greatly and the sun was blocked by the clouds, which was the exact thing Chris needed to cool off. It was obvious that rain was about to fall, so Josh and I jumped into action to set up the tents quickly, helping Chris set up his tent first, and then setting up our own.

The map indicated a potential water source a few

hundred yards north of camp. Having his tent set up before mine, Josh set out alone in the general direction with an empty water container. A long twenty minutes later, he walked into camp with a Nalgene full of water, handed it to Chris, and then both Josh and I went back to refill the rest of our containers.

***

Thunder echoed across the canyon walls and wind blew dust through the air, but there was no rain to be seen. Over the next four to five hours, we alternated between sitting around camp and laying in our tents.

The one luxury we had for the first time in three days was an actual toilet. The campsite had a vault toilet in the form of a small outhouse. Josh was the first to venture in, and when he came out, he reported it was the best bathroom experience he ever had. Thinking he was joking or that the heat was making him delusional, I then walked over and occupied the toilet myself. To my delight, it did not smell like most outhouses do. Leaving the door open, as Josh said to do, the view of the canyon was magnificent. It was without a doubt the best view I'd ever seen from a toilet.

Unbeknown to us at the time, a flash flood watch was in effect for our location that afternoon and for the overnight. Even without the knowledge, we still set up camp high above the dry creek bed as a precaution since rain appeared imminent. But once the sun set, we went to bed without even seeing a single drop of rain.

That night, the sound of rain hitting my tent woke me up in the wee hours of the morning, but I quickly fell back asleep. Waking up again at 5:00 A.M. to the sound of my alarm, the light steady rain had unfortunately turned into a heavy downpour. Josh called out asking if I was awake, saying he had been up since 4:30 and it had been pouring the entire time.

With a five-mile hike to the car, followed by a seven-hour drive to Southwest Utah, our plan was to get a very early start that morning. But with the heavy rain, we waited thirty minutes in hopes it would slow or stop, but it never did; so we broke down our tents and packed our gear in the cool sixty-degree rain.

The best way to break down a tent in the rain is to do it from the inside out. While sitting inside the tent, I unclipped the tent from the poles while leaving the rain cover clipped in. This allowed me to pack all my gear, including my tent, from underneath the rain cover. After my pack was loaded and I donned my rain gear and pack cover, I broke down the rain cover and tent poles.

My gear got a little wet, but was far from soaked, and most importantly we were able to keep our clothes and bodies dry. Wasting no time, we were moving on the trail as soon as we packed up; and no more than five minutes later, the rain stopped.

While looking at the map the previous evening, a potential alternative route back to the car was found. There was a Jeep trail that led directly to a dirt road, which then provided a straight shot to the main road. We felt we could all hike to the Jeep trail/dirt road intersection and then leave Chris there, while Josh and I retrieved the car.

With Chris still not feeling well that morning, and with the added hazardous weather threat, we felt hiking the main trail over steep slickrock canyon walls wasn't in our best interest.

The hike on the Jeep trail was completely flat. When we reached the dirt road, Chris agreed to stay put (with our distress beacon) while Josh and I dropped our packs and started running/walking the 3.7 miles down the road to retrieve the car.

Having made it about halfway to the car, we heard a vehicle coming up behind us. Noticing the vehicle was a law enforcement ranger, we flagged them down, and after talking to the ranger and explaining our situation, she kindly provided us a ride back to our car. We hopped in the car and met Chris a few minutes later.

The remainder of the day was spent in the car driving six to seven hours to St. George, Utah. Chris slept most of the way and still felt a little unwell that night.

A year after the trip, during a medical training event, I learned that when urine changes colors from dark brown to completely clear in such a short time frame, that it is most likely a bad sign - a possible indication of hyponatremia, which is basically when your body no longer contains enough sodium. When this happens, your body tries to expel excess water in an attempt to preserve the sodium it has left.

Back on the trail, when Chris drank the liter of water while we were resting, his body almost immediately expelled it. Even though we gave him the electrolyte mix, his body needed a lot more sodium and other electrolytes than what was in the one packet.

While we are unsure what his condition was, since both hyponatremia and heat exhaustion exhibit the symptoms he had, we felt we made the best decision by stopping to rest and then turning around to camp another night.

ZION NATIONAL PARK

The drive from Canyonlands National Park to St. George, Utah was very scenic. Our route took us through Monument Valley, across Glen Canyon Dam, and through Grand Staircase-Escalante National Monument.

We were looking forward to sleeping in a hotel, taking a shower, and soaking in a pool after four days in the wilderness. We were also looking forward to a hot, fresh meal, and ended up at a Texas Roadhouse eating a lot more food than we should have. We thankfully enjoyed a comfortable evening, as we were about to spend another two days in the wilderness.

Before bed that evening, we had to re-pack and re-supply our gear for the next day's backpacking trip. The trek into The Narrows would be completely different than the Canyonlands hike. Located in Zion National Park, the trail is deep inside a canyon with walls of over 1,000 feet on both sides of the trail.

The trail itself is primarily in the Virgin River with the river spanning the entire width of the canyon in many sections, and therefore no dry land between the sheer canyon walls. One such section is more than a mile long, providing no means of escape in the event of a flash flood.

With the hike being a one-way trek, we had a shuttle scheduled for 9:30 A.M. to take us to the top of The Narrows at Chamberlain's Ranch; then we would hike a total of sixteen miles over the next two days, stopping to camp at campsite #9.

Similar to Canyonlands National Park, we were required to check-in and pick up our permit prior to starting the hike, so we arrived early the next morning at the Zion National Park visitor center.

Walking through the visitor center and over to the wilderness desk, we noticed multiple signs indicating dangerous hiking conditions. Specifically, flash flood watches were in effect, and the flash flood danger in the park was considered very high. The rangers issuing our permit asked if we were aware of the danger and reiterated that many people had died in previous years from flash floods.

They said a flash flood may occur quickly and without warning, even under sunny skies; a storm could produce heavy rainfall many miles away, and since the runoff must go somewhere, it could cause a flash flood for locations many miles downstream, including The Narrows.

The rangers said it was our decision as to hike or not, as the park would not close the trail unless a flash flood was occurring. I hypothetically asked both rangers a question: if they had been planning to complete the hike, just as we were, would they continue as planned? Both rangers responded that they would not go, as the threat was very real and because there were many locations on the trail that offered no escape from a flood.

I'd been looking forward to this hike for over six months and knew it may be my only opportunity to complete it. But I also knew from years of experience that weather was unpredictable and had the ability to be deadly. So, after some deliberation, we ultimately decided to forgo our plans.

Even though he tried to hide it, Chris appeared relieved. He would have absolutely gone on the hike without objection, but it was apparent that he still was not feeling well.

Our first stop after leaving the visitor center was at the Zion Adventure Company, with whom we arranged our shuttle. Just like the Moab shuttle, we had pre-paid for the ride; however, the Zion Adventure Company had much more regard for our well-being, and with the flash flood threat being very real, they provided us with a full $111 refund even though it was outside of their cancellation window.

We then had to figure out where we would sleep that night since we were no longer camping in The Narrows. Driving through the two campgrounds located near the entrance of Zion, they were both very crowded. With all of the hotels in Springdale fully booked, which usually occurs months in advance, we drove out of town and turned onto Kolob Terrace Road. Not too far up the road was an empty Bureau of Land Management (BLM) campground. We pulled in and found a great campsite nestled against North Creek, so we unpacked our gear, set up our tents, and then headed back into Zion for some day hiking.

Unlike the middle section of The Narrows, the lower section offered many places to climb to safety in the event of a flood and was very accessible to day hikers. After we arrived back to the visitor center, we boarded a Zion park bus and rode to the trailhead; the same location we had planned to end our hike while backpacking.

The first couple miles were very crowded, but soon we lost the crowds and gained the solitude I was seeking. Hiking upstream through the river was unlike any hike or anything we had ever seen. Deep inside the canyon, with sheer walls towering over 1,000 feet, the crystal-clear water wound its way around large bends and boulders.

I wanted to hike the entire day through the knee and waist deep river, and was regretting the decision to forgo the backpacking. Looking up, nothing but blue sky and sunshine was present. Setting up camp on the riverbed at the bottom of the canyon would have been serene and picturesque.

But the threat of a flash flood was still on our mind. With an overabundance of caution, we kept an eye out for any signs of an impending flood. Warning signs such as the water turning cloudy, small debris floating downstream, or a thundering roar coming from up-canyon could indicate a flash flood was about to occur. The warnings may have only appeared a minute before a flood but could have given us a fair shot at reaching higher ground. Thankfully, we never saw or heard any of these warning signs, but as soon as we noticed some dark clouds building above us, we turned around and headed back to the trailhead.

Making our way back to town, we sat down for a late lunch at the Zion Canyon Brewing Company and talked about our camping plans for the evening, such as what food we wanted for dinner (we didn't want our freeze-dried food) and if we wanted to purchase some firewood. Hot and sweaty from day hiking, and still sore and tired from the Canyonlands backpacking, we slowly talked ourselves out of wanting to camp that night.

An online search showed the closest available hotel was in St. George, and by the time we finished lunch, we agreed to drive forty-five minutes back to the city and stay in a hotel, with a quick detour to pack up our tents from the BLM campground.

Chris and Josh hiking in The Narrows

***

Zion National Park becomes crowded very quickly, and the hike we planned to attempt the next morning was one of the most popular. Trail descriptions indicated the Angels Landing trail was a strenuous uphill hike, climbing 1,600 feet in 2.2 miles. Once near the top, the trail was only wide enough for one person, with narrow sections exposing hikers to sheer drops of over 1,000 feet.

In one section, the trail was reported to be no more than three feet wide, flanked on both sides by a sheer drop. Because of the exposure, the park service had placed chains on this and other sections of the trail for safety and for a little peace of mind. The narrow trail, along with the high, remote summit, was what gave this mesa its name. In 1916, an explorer named Frederick Fisher said, "Angels Landing is so high that only an angel could land on it."

In an attempt to beat the crowds, we had another early morning drive to the park, where we boarded a shuttle bus at 7:00 A.M. Arriving at the trailhead a few minutes later, and then commencing our hike soon after, we were joined by a slew of other hikers.

The initial half mile was a steady and easily manageable uphill trail, followed by about a mile of steep and long switchbacks. The trail then climbed through a canyon and became even steeper, so much that we had to stop every five minutes to catch our breath.

At last, we made it to the famous switchbacks, which were the shortest and tightest switchbacks I'd ever seen. Each direction we walked only eight or so steps before turning back the other direction, for a total of twenty-one switchbacks.

Immediately following the switchbacks, we arrived at an opening named Scout Lookout. From here, the narrow ridge leading all the way to the top of Angels Landing was visible, and the visually intimidating path resulted in many hikers ending their hike at the lookout.

We continued the final half-mile of trail to the top via a steep and very exposed path. There were times we had to wait a few minutes for hikers to come down a section of trail before we could continue up, since there was not enough room for two people to pass one another.

On the summit of Angels Landing, we were awarded with an amazing panoramic view of the canyon. There were at least thirty other people on the summit, and looking back down the trail we saw what looked like hundreds of others coming our way.

The hike down the exposed ridge to Scout Lookout took twice as long as the hike up. The trail was clogged with hikers, and we frequently had to wait upwards of ten minutes to allow large groups of people to come up the trail. But once we made it off the ridge and onto Scout Lookout, we hastily hiked down the switchbacks to get away from the large crowd; and soon after reached the trailhead.

Packed into a standing room only shuttle bus, we rode back to the visitor center, then jumped into our car and hit the road. Our destination was Salt Lake City, as our flight back home to Georgia was scheduled for the following morning.

Josh hiking up Angels Landing

***

After a quick stay in Salt Lake City that evening, our first wilderness trip to Utah was in the books. We even started planning our next trip while traveling back home. While we encountered a few set-backs and many changes in plans, we thoroughly enjoyed the trip.

Similar to many of my adventures back home, the weather played a big factor throughout the trip. The heavy rains in Canyonlands prevented us from reaching the trailhead, and the threat of flash floods prevented us from completing our Zion backpacking portion of the trip.

In hindsight, since no flood occurred, we regretted our decision not to backpack The Narrows. Why did we make that decision and was it the right decision? That is a question I still ask myself and wonder if I would make the same decision today.

Part of the answer is we were dealing with many unknowns, such as never having hiked the trail, never having hiked in a deep, inescapable canyon, and never having experienced a flash flood.

Today, with not as many unknowns, I might decide to do the backpacking trek in the same conditions. But while I may feel safer and more prepared, those feelings don't actually reduce the risk of dying from a flash flood.

Three months after the trip, in September 2015, twenty people died in flash floods in the same region of Utah, including seven hikers in Zion National Park. Most of these people where experienced hikers and were hiking locations they were familiar with.

Why were these hikers exploring slot canyons during a flash flood watch? Maybe they felt comfortable and that there were no unknowns or things outside of their control. Maybe they had the trip planned for over a year and didn't want to back-out or change the plan due to a small chance of a flood. Maybe they had backed-out of many trips before due to a flood risk that never materialized, and therefore stopped heeding the warning.

Before making any decision today, I ask myself "What

can I control and what can I not?". And then I ask, "Of the things I cannot control, what are the consequences if they happen and how can I mitigate it?". Thoroughly examining these questions can mean the difference in life or death on any wilderness adventure.

EXTREME HEAT

In 2021, the opportunity to backpack and camp in The Narrows was presented again. Similar to my previous attempt, this trip was planned for mid-June near the start of monsoon season.

Keeping a keen eye on the weather leading up to the trip, the primary hazard was not a flash flood, as there was no rain in the forecast, but rather the extreme heat was of concern. Forecasted highs were around 110 degrees for the entire trip – higher than I have ever experienced in my life.

The body can acclimate to heat over a process taking multiple weeks, but I had been couped up working inside almost every day leading up to the trip. I made it outside a few times walking, running, and biking in the ninety-degree, humid, Georgia heat, but it wasn't nearly enough to fully acclimate to extreme heat. I wasn't worried however, knowing The Narrows hike was primarily walking through knee deep, sixty-degree water, and the deep, narrow slot canyon would keep temperatures a little cooler than the forecast.

I was meeting a group of five others, four of whom were backpacking the Grand Canyon rim-to-rim a couple days prior to our Narrows trip. Exposed to the sun, hiking on steep terrain, carrying heavy packs with food and supplies for three days, and with extreme heat, it was essential to not only drink a lot of water but to consume supplemental electrolytes and the correct types of food — those high in calories, salt, and light in weight.

Two of the women in the group had never backpacked before and had relied on the trip leader's extensive recommendations for pre-trip planning, packing lists, heat acclimation, and physical conditioning for months leading up to the trip. With the two inexperienced women living in different parts of the country, all of the pre-trip planning and packing was done remotely through emails, texts, and phone calls. The trip leader, Aubri, and her colleague were both wilderness medicine and outdoor adventure experts, so the quality of recommendations provided were excellent.

In her email to the group, Aubri provided the following considerations for food to pack:

"oatmeal packets/powerbars for breakfast + instant coffee/tea/pourover coffee

Nuts/powerbars/pita bread&spread/cheese/jerky/tortillas or wraps with PBJ for lunches

Freeze dried meals/ramen/easymac/instant mashed potatoes for dinners

Nuts/powerbars/dried fruit/jerky/runner's gels/gummies for snacks

Electrolyte tabs to add to water (Nuun, IV hydration powder, etc)"

When everyone arrived in Las Vegas the evening before the hike, a gear check was performed to ensure everyone had the correct gear and food. While looking at one of the hiker's food supply, immediate concern was raised. Rather than the freeze-dried meals that were suggested, she had packed frozen dinners that had been defrosted and re-packed into Ziplock bags. In addition, she packed hard-boiled eggs, 4 pounds of apples, hummus, and celery. Her meals were a recipe for food poisoning - cooked food spoils rapidly at 120 degrees. Additionally, they contained very little calories, little to no electrolytes, and were excessively heavy. Pre-planning for such a scenario, Aubri and her colleague had enough extra food to provide to her for the trip.

It was an early Sunday morning that they dropped into the canyon from the North Rim. The temperature was a frigid thirty degrees, but rose rapidly to 120 degrees before reaching the bottom of the canyon. The rim-to-rim trek took two nights and three days, and consisted of just as much hiking in the pre-dawn darkness as it did in the day. The only way to avoid the excessive heat and sun was to hike during the night, and with a clearly marked trail, the national park recommends not hiking from 10:00 A.M. to 4:00 P.M. in excessive heat.

Completing the hike at the South Rim a few hours after sunrise Tuesday morning, they were all proud and excited to have completed such an intense trek. Very tired, very hot, and ready for a short break before dropping into The Narrows two days later, they rested for the remainder of the day and then headed to Zion on Wednesday.

***

I arrived in Springdale Wednesday afternoon and checked-in with the Zion Wilderness Desk to pick up our backpacking permit. Walking three miles through town in the 110-degree heat was exhausting and unlike any heat I have ever experienced. Since the first three miles of backpacking the next day would be on dry land with no shade, I was anxious to get an early start to beat the heat. But with none of the five group members in town yet by 6:00 P.M., I was not optimistic of getting an early start.

When Aubri and her colleague arrived that evening, we repacked their backpacks and came up with a plan for the following morning: we'd plan to depart Springdale around 8:30 A.M. and be at the trailhead by 10:00, much later than I desired. The reason for the late start was the other three women coming on the trip had car trouble in Arizona and wouldn't arrive to town until after midnight. To ensure adequate rest and enough time to check everyone's gear in the morning, 8:30 was as early as we could reasonably shoot for.

A difficult decision the morning of the hike was determining how much water to carry. We had twelve miles to cover in the dry desert heat, yet we'd be walking through water for most of those miles. But drinking water from the river was completely out of the picture.

A warning advisory indicating the presence of cyanobacteria and cyanotoxins in the water was in effect for the river. With no known recreational water filtration methods effective at clearing water of cyanotoxins, including iodine tablets and boiling water, we had to rely on natural springs to re-fill our water. Knowing this in advance, I asked the ranger at the Zion Wilderness Desk if there would be any reliable springs other than Big Springs (around mile 12 and near our campsite). He responded that there were springs were abundant in the area and we shouldn't have any issue finding water. Armed with this knowledge, I decided to carry 3.5 liters, and most of the others packed around four liters.

When we departed the Chamberlains Ranch trailhead at 10:30 A.M., we were lucky to have an overcast sky and temperatures in the upper eighties. The first three miles went by quickly and we stepped into the North Fork of the Virgin River around the same time the sun appeared in full force. It didn't take long for the temperature to break a hundred degrees and suddenly we all slowed our pace, took frequent breaks, and began drinking more water.

The walls of the canyon became steeper, taller, and the river narrowed over the next few miles – there were points where we could stretch out our arms and touch both walls of the deep canyon at the same time. Our pace slowed dramatically. The scenery was extraordinary. Constantly turning around to see the canyon from both angles, looking up at the endless walls, and taking pictures of the most scenic backpacking trail I've ever hiked put us a good one hour behind schedule by the time we reached the beginning of campsites at mile nine. We only had three miles left to hike, but I knew those miles were the most difficult and would take us upwards of three hours to complete.

The temperature had fallen noticeably when we entered the narrow canyon. But even though the temperature was in the upper seventies, we still needed to drink a lot of water due to the dry air and physical exertion. We all kept a lookout for one of the abundant springs the ranger told me about, be none were found. I was down to my last liter, Aubri to her last half liter, and others running low as well. We had to push on though if we wanted to get to the campsite before dark.

Hiking in the dark would have been very dangerous. The river had no defined trail and required a lot of route planning based on upcoming obstacles such as boulders or deep pools; the river also had a lot of bowling ball sized boulders that made for dangerous footing which would be amplified in darkness; the campsites were not marked clearly and it was not obvious when a side trail led to a campsite – I'm not sure I would have been able to find the site in the dark.

Using my pre-downloaded map, I could tell we were getting close to the campsite, which was a welcome relief as Aubri and I were both out of water. We had constantly been on the lookout for a spring since the ranger said they were abundant, but we couldn't find any (the region was in an exceptional drought at the time and the river flow was around all time lows).

I was the first to reach camp and had an unexpected surprise awaiting my arrival. As soon as I walked into camp, I noticed there was hiking gear and a hammock set up. Not wanting to surprise someone in the very remote area, I called out from a distance to announce my presence. That's when I saw the arms of a man reach out of the hammock and grab a pair of underwear. Believing he was butt naked in his hammock, I waited a couple minutes to give him time to put some clothes on.

I was not happy at all. We had a permit secured for this campsite, which was very difficult to secure, and yet here was a naked man who decided to set up camp for himself in our site. As soon as I walked up to him, I asked if he had a permit for the site. He said, "No. I have a permit for site eleven, but I couldn't find the site. But when I asked the rangers yesterday when I got my permit, they said this site would be empty."

I informed him that he was wrong, that there was no room for him at our site, and that he would need to leave. He wasn't happy about it, but we weren't going to share our already cramped space with him – especially since he was naked when I arrived, obviously lied about the conversation with the rangers, and I doubt he missed his campsite. Based on the circumstances, we were pretty certain he day-hiked from the exit point to our site (which is the first site he would have seen) and he hoped no one would show up.

Once our unexpected intruder departed, we walked a few hundred yards to Big Springs to finally refill our water. The spring was a waterfall coming directly out of the canyon wall and was flowing well. We filled up at least ten bottles and took them back to camp to treat using iodine tablets.

The Portable Aqua tablets come in two similar looking containers – one container with iodine tablets for purification and the other with neutralizing tablets to remove the iodine taste. Back at camp with full water containers, we were all very thirsty, hungry, tired, and sore, but we had to keep working to set up camp, make dinner, and purify water. Rather than taking the time to do both of the Portable Aqua tablets, it was decided to only use the iodine tablet. Tablets were placed into each liter of water and then twenty minutes later were ready to drink. As soon as mine was ready, I drank almost half a liter.

Later that night when I was in the tent, I made a comment that the water didn't taste like iodine and asked if we had used the neutralizing tablets as well. Concern quickly grew when the realization hit that we indeed had not used the iodine tablets, but rather only the neutralizing tablets. I immediately stopped drinking the water, put a sodium chlorite tablet into my other water bottle to purify overnight (those tablets take four hours before the water is safe to drink), and then went to sleep hoping not to wake up sick the next morning.

The next morning no one was sick and we all re-purified our water with either iodine or sodium chlorite, and then hit the trail before 9:00 A.M. The hike out that day was very scenic. Again, we were hiking though water for the majority of the hike, some of which was chest deep, keeping us cool from the increasing temperature. Unfortunately, the crowds that we encountered over the last couple miles were heavy. We passed at least a thousand people before we made it to the trail exit, removing any sense of being in the wilderness from my mind.

Over the next week there was some concern of getting sick from drinking the non-purified water, but we felt the water source was very safe as the water was flowing heavily and directly out of the canyon wall (I do not recommend drinking from this spring or any spring without purifying the water first). Thankfully, no one ever got sick.

The hike was more difficult than I had anticipated, and we almost made a detrimental mistake by not bringing enough water. If we had been camping at one of the sites a mile or more upstream from Big Springs, we wouldn't have had enough water for dinner, overnight, and the next morning. Two of us - paired for safety reasons - would have needed to hike all the way to Big Springs to fill up all the water bottles for the group.

In fact, another group camping at one of the earlier campsites had to spend the night with only a liter of water between their group of 5 hikers and wait to make breakfast until they reached Big Springs the following morning.

Prior to the hike I was so concerned with my pack weight that I didn't want any additional weight by adding more water. My pack had only weighed twenty-five pounds, so it was completely unreasonable for me not to go ahead and carry an extra liter. I will not make that mistake again, especially in the desert during an excessive heat warning and an exceptional drought. Overall, the trip was a success, and even though I've now completed the most iconic hikes in Zion, there are still even more canyoneering and backpacking routes I desire to explore in the park.

The author backpacking in The Narrows

7 - THE RED PLANET

<u>TRIP PLANNING</u>

The Utah trip in 2015 provided us with many ideas for our 2016 trip. Our limited time in Moab had left us wanting to see more of the town, and as much as we enjoyed the four-day backpacking trek in Canyonlands, we were left with little time to explore other areas. Seeking more time to hike and explore areas around Moab, we decided to limit our backpacking to a one-night trek in 2016.

Weather was a big factor on the 2015 trip, and in an attempt to avoid the hot summer heat, we planned our 2016 trip for late March and into early April - the average high for Moab in March is about thirty degrees cooler than June, coming in at sixty-four degrees.

As we experienced in 2015, traveling to Moab required a lot of driving due to its remote location and lack of a commercial airport. The major airports closest to Moab are Salt Lake City - about a four-hour drive away - and Denver - about 5.5 hours away. Having flown into Salt

Lake City in 2015, and with Josh and Chris having never traveled to Colorado, we planned to fly to Denver and then drive to Moab.

Despite our plan to spend only one night backpacking, I still had a desire to camp rather than stay in a hotel the other nights. I researched areas around Moab and took notice of the Arches National Park campground, Devils Garden. According to many websites, the campground typically booked up many months in advance. So, in late 2015, I went ahead and made a reservation for a Tuesday night in late March 2016.

With the Arches reservation secured, we needed to focus on planning our backpacking trek. Backpacking through the Needles District was amazing the previous year, and with a shared affinity to the landscape and environment, we planned our one-night backpacking trek in the same general area as before.

Through online research and studying topo maps, I found an area in the Needles District called Chesler Park with five reservable backcountry campsites. Applying for the highly sought after CP1 campsite, literally the minute the reservation system opened for the date we were seeking, we secured our permit for the six to seven-mile round trip hike.

In addition to Arches National Park and the Canyonlands Needles District, we planned to visit both the Island in the Sky District of Canyonlands and the San Rafael Swell. The San Rafael Swell, being located on BLM land, offered many open camping opportunities, and our plan was to find an area off a dirt road to camp for one night.

The final itinerary included three nights of camping and five nights of hotels, which was the same amount of camping as our 2015 trip.

A month before the trip, Josh sent out a lengthy, yet detailed email to the group; which I now keep as a packing guide for all of my wilderness trips.

Josh's Email, Feb 15, 2016:

Western Adventure Part II
3/25 - 4/2
Colorado/Utah Packing List:

GEAR
- *Tent*
- *Large Back Pack*
- *Secondary Smaller Day Pack (Packed inside other, larger pack for flight out)*
- *Sleeping Bag (20 degree rated or below)*
- *Sleeping Bag Liner*
- *Sleeping Pad*
- *Pillow*
- *Dry Bags x 3*
- *Toilet paper*
- *Baby wipes*
- *Hand sanitizer*
- *Toothbrush/paste*
- *Water bottles x 2*
- *CamelBak Bladder*
- *Water Treatment tabs (emergency) *Should be able to carry water w/o sourcing our own**
- *Jet Boil/MSR (I might not even take mine or we could all share)*
- *Fuel (buy in Denver)*
- *Spork*
- *Knife*
- *Lighter*
- *Duct Tape*

o   *Head lamp*
o   *Flashlight (back up)*
o   *Whistle/Compass*
o   *Handkerchief/ Small Towel/ Cloth*
o   *Sun Glasses*
o   *Camera*
o   *Ibuprofen*
o   *Benadryl*
o   *Imodium*
o   *Band aids*
o   *Hand Warmers (can also throw into sleeping bag at night)*

We'll only have one day of camping not near the car, so carrying water and food [is] not really an issue. Most of our gear can be stored in the car while we hike except for the first camping night, Sunday 3/27.

For Sunday in Utah we will need to carry all of our water and food to [the] campsite, about 4 miles from [the] car/trailhead [and] then 4 miles back in the morning.

CLOTHES
o   *Winter Fleeced Lined Coat*
o   *Waterproof (NF/ Mtn Hardware or Similar) *night**
o   *Lighter Layering jacket/coat/fleece*
o   *Gloves*
o   *Beanie*
o   *Warm hiking socks x 5*
o   *Sleeping socks*
o   *Durable Hiking Pants x 2*
o   *Sweat pants (cotton) to sleep in*
o   *Long Sleeve Shirt for Sleeping*
o   *Gym Shorts*
o   *T-Shirts/Day Shirts*

- ○ *Hat*
- ○ *Hiking Boots*
- ○ *Town Clothes (pants/shirts/shoes/socks/etc)*
- ○ *Underoos*

As for sleeping in relatively cool/cold weather at night, I've found it's much more comfortable to wear sweatpants and a loose cotton shirt and socks as opposed to synthetic "Under Armor" style "Cold Gear" clothes, they are very constricting and uncomfortable and impossible to get out of if you get hot at night.

Temperatures during the day should be in the mid to low 60's but at that higher Colorado elevation it can change quickly, so prepare for possible cold weather. Nights will be cooler/cold especially in the Utah desert. I've slept outside when it's in the teens at 6,000 feet in a 20 [degree] bag w/ a liner and survived. It won't be nearly that cold plus a tent greatly helps trap the warmth. Throw a few hand warmers in the bottom of your bag and it's all good.

FOOD
- ○ *Cliff Bars/Energy Snack Bars*
- ○ *Water*
- ○ *Electrolyte Tabs/Powder*
- ○ *Jerky/Trail Mix/Snacks*
- ○ *Coffee/Tea Packets*
- ○ *Candy/Snickers*
- ○ *Freeze Dried Meal Possibly*
- ○ *Sport Beans*

Again we really only have one day/night where we have to carry all of our food and water and that's the first night we go camping/hiking on Sunday. The other nights we can eat by the car so we can have whatever food we want plus plenty of water/Gatorade in the car. Otherwise it's just snacks and energy bars for our hiking during the day and lunch.

MISCELLANEOUS
- ○ *Wallet*
- ○ *Cash*
- ○ *Phone/Charger*
- ○ *Permits*
- ○ *Maps*
- ○ *Guide Book*
- ○ *Personal Meds i.e. Allergy/Contacts/etc.*
- ○ *Camp Shoes (Croc's)*
- ○ *Watch*
- ○ *Carry on/ Hotel bag and Toiletries*
- ○ *Sunscreen*
- ○ *Large Bag for Backpack Checked Baggage*

CANYONLANDS NATIONAL PARK

Our flight departed early Friday morning from Atlanta, arriving in Denver a few hours later. Walking out of the Denver airport, the air was cold and patches of snow were on the ground. The weather forecast called for more snow over the next twenty-four hours, so we wasted no time picking up our rental car and hitting the road.

The main highway heading west out of Denver, Interstate 70, climbed up to the continental divide before tunneling directly under it. The Eisenhower tunnel, at 11,158 feet above sea level, is the highest vehicular tunnel in the world. It is also the highest point on any US Interstate, so it is easy to imagine how often the road near the tunnel is impacted by snow, with complete road closures possible during some snowstorms.

A combination of Friday afternoon traffic and snow showers clogged the road with stop-and-go traffic. By the time we reached the tunnel, heavy snow was falling, slowing us to a five-mile-per-hour pace. But once through the tunnel, the sun was shining as the highway quickly dropped thousands of feet, and we drove another couple hours to stay in Grand Junction that evening.

Saturday morning, we headed into Utah and went straight to Canyonlands National Park, Island in the Sky district. Parking at the Upheaval Dome trailhead, we stretched our legs, loaded our packs with plenty of water and snacks, and set out on a long and difficult day hike.

The Syncline Loop, originating at the same location as the Upheaval Dome trail, was our goal for the mostly sunny, yet very cold day. We were thankful for the cold weather, which made for much better hiking conditions than the ninety to one-hundred-degree temperatures we experienced the previous year. Wearing light jackets, gloves, and beanies, we began the hike heading counterclockwise; and then quickly removed those garments and continued in short sleeves and long pants for the remainder of the hike.

Rated as a very strenuous trail and with no access to water, each of us carried a heavy four liters of water in our daypacks. In addition to water, I packed my standard day hiking supplies that included snacks, a first aid kit, compass, knife, satellite distress beacon, space blanket, paracord, map, solar charger, and sunscreen.

The trail started at the top of a canyon, descended over 1,500 feet to the canyon floor, and then climbed back up to the top; making for an 8.4-mile loop.

After a few miles of hiking, we made it to our final descent into the canyon. The trail almost completely disappeared from the steep, rocky slope, requiring route finding and some scrambling over and around many boulders.

I was having a great time and was very happy with the hike we chose - the views were wonderous, open, and far-reaching; the seclusion was apparent with the lack of other hikers, the stillness, and the quietness of the area; the freedom of being disconnected from the outside world was felt; the difficulty of the hike required navigation and route finding skills, and presented us with both physically demanding and dangerous terrain. Everything I sought on our weeklong trip was already being fulfilled on the first half of our first hike.

Reaching the bottom of the canyon, the trail changed its character and became straight, flat, and easy to follow for a couple of miles. We were feeling great and enjoying the hike, until we noticed the canyon wall we had to climb to get out of the canyon.

The steep canyon wall looked impossible to hike up from our vantage point at the bottom. While we stopped to rest at the base of the climb, eating energy bars and staying hydrated, we debated which route the trail would take up the wall.

Pushing forward, the climb out was grueling, as the trail climbed 1,075 feet over 1.1 miles. As we reached the top, we were sweating and winded, and it felt like we were hiking in the summer desert heat again; although we quickly realized it was still very cold when snow began to fall.

The last mile back to the car was easy. We passed many hikers exploring Upheaval Dome, all of whom gave us weird looks; probably wondering how we were hiking in short sleeves in the cold, windy, and snowy conditions. With the hike complete, I knew I was not nearly in as good physical condition as I was the previous year. The hike out of the canyon winded me quickly and my legs were burning the entire time. In the car ride to Moab, I could feel the soreness setting in my legs. I didn't mention anything at the time, as I didn't want to appear as the weak link, but I'd soon find out it wasn't just me who didn't physically prepare well enough for the trip.

Searching for the route to the canyon floor

***

Back in Moab for the second time in less than a year, we checked in to our hotel and prepared our gear for the next day's backpacking trek in the Needles District. Similar to the Syncline Loop, there would be no water sources on the entire hike, and being in the wilderness for twenty-four hours, we had to guess as to the right amount of water we'd need. Since the temperatures were mild, not getting out of the sixties, we settled on packing five liters each; weighing my pack down with eleven pounds of water.

Doing our best to remove all non-essential and redundant items from our packs, my pack still weighed about ten pounds more than I was hoping, coming in at around forty pounds. But the hike to the campsite was short, just over three miles, so we were not too concerned; and depending on weather conditions, we could possibly dump some excess water out on the hike back to the car.

After an hour drive from Moab, we left our car at the crowded Elephant Hill parking lot and began our hike up a steep path. The initial section of trail consisted of many switchbacks and climbed a few hundred feet in elevation.

We had been hiking no more than fifteen minutes when we all became winded and sweaty. Stopping to catch our breath, we looked down the path and could still see the parking lot and our car. We knew how pitiful we were at that moment - unable to get out of sight of the car before we had to stop and rest. While I felt dispirited, it was a relief seeing both Chris and Josh just as exhausted as I was.

In addition to poor physical conditioning leading up to the trip, the effects of our strenuous hike the day before coupled with our heavier than usual packs were weighing on us. Hindsight told me we should have completed the backpacking portion of our trip before attempting the Syncline Loop day hike.

If not for the ensuing embarrassment, I think we would have agreed to turn around, go back to the car, and just camp in the park's campground. But with many other people hiking past us, some with heavy packs on just like us, we were not going to become the laughingstock of the trail. Concealing our struggle as best we could, we continued on the almost entirely uphill trail.

Taking an unreasonably long two hours to hike the three miles, we followed the signs to the CP1 campsite and set up camp. Hidden from the main trail, we found solitude in the cool, dry, and dusty desert environment. The site was flanked by a large wall to the north and east, and by a very large stack of boulders to the south. A break in the north wall provided a viewpoint perched high above the canyon floor, where we gazed at the far-reaching and diverse view comprised of canyons, mesas, desert, and snow-covered mountain peaks.

With camp set up and the desire to go explore, we threw on our daypacks and set out on a late afternoon hike on the Joint Trail. One of the most fascinating trails I've ever hiked, the trail was at the bottom of a very narrow slot canyon. As we walked through the narrow crack, portions of the trail were so tight that I could touch both walls of the canyon with my shoulders simultaneously. Fascinated by the unordinary formations, we explored slots off the main trail that required us to squeeze our bodies sideways through the canyon.

With the sun making its way lower on the horizon and light dwindling inside the slots, we hiked through the open, still, and silent desert back to camp.

Dinner that night was simple. I didn't want to weigh my pack down with my camping stove, fuel, extra water, or a pot, and therefore needed a meal that didn't require cooking or heating water. So, I packed tortilla shells, peanut butter, and jelly, and prepared a few PB&J tacos while sitting on the edge of the cliff just north of camp. They were delicious, full of calories, easy to pack, and easy to prepare.

The view from our campsite of the western horizon was unobstructed, and as soon as the sun touched the horizon, the sky, the desert floor, and the surrounding spires and cliffs all turned fiery red. The sunset was unrivaled by any other, with rays of light casting outward across the entire sky. Colors ranged from red, purple, blue, and pink; and with the ideal level of moisture in the air, the clouds and clear sky contrasted with each other perfectly. Wearing beanies, gloves, and thick jackets, we admired the magnificent sunset in the secluded, inhospitable desert.

The next morning was cold, and I didn't want to get out of my warm sleeping bag. After waking up slowly, we had a leisurely morning while we ate breakfast and broke down camp. Back on the trail and carrying only one liter of water each, the almost entirely downhill hike was quick. We arrived at the car before noon and headed to Moab to explore the town and freshen up at a hotel.

MARS AND THE SWELL

A few days after our backpacking trek, we planned to drive towards Hanksville and explore the San Rafael Swell, go see what it would be like to live on the Red Planet, and then find a place to camp on BLM land. The areas we were traveling to were very desolate, so we filled up on gas, downloaded some maps on our phones, and made our way to our first stop, Mars.

Josh and Chris were adamant that we attempt to locate the Mars Desert Research Station, located somewhere off a barren dirt road in an area that resembled Mars. Josh became aware of the facility while studying the San Rafael Swell using Google Earth imagery. He noticed some interesting structures in the middle of nowhere, and upon further examination, saw it was a Mars Society facility.

Without directions to follow, all we had were the aerial images and our GPS. We turned off the paved road and onto a BLM dirt road that appeared to lead the way. After a few miles of driving, with absolutely no signs of civilization besides the road, we turned a corner and saw the facility.

A sight to behold was a Mars base consisting of six structures including a living structure. We walked around the base and looked out over the landscape. Not a single tree, plant, bush, twig, or anything resembling life was within sight; nothing but red and white rocks and dirt.

Besides the atmosphere and temperature, the environment was very similar to that on Mars, which is why the location was chosen for the facility. We didn't see any of the inhabitants, nor did we try to bother them, as these were researchers and scientists studying the best ways for humans to live on Mars.

With the San Rafael Swell nearby, we left Mars and drove to a popular trailhead. Parking at the trailhead next to at least ten other cars, we hiked the Little Wildhorse Canyon trail. Slot canyons with walls rising over a hundred feet made up half the hike. A few technical sections required scrambling over boulders, but otherwise, the hike was easy and well shaded in the slots.

It was early afternoon when we finished the hike and our only remaining plan for the day was to camp. I was excited to make camp and then do nothing but enjoy the desert solitude. The weather looked decent - not as cold as the previous night, but there was a slight chance of a passing shower.

When we drove to the trailhead earlier, we passed many spots off the BLM road that looked suitable for camping. But as soon as we started driving back down the road, Josh, out of nowhere, said he'd rather not camp; he'd rather go back to Moab and stay in a hotel instead. He sounded serious, but I hoped he was joking. Chris then chimed in, agreeing that hanging out in Moab and sleeping in a hotel sounded good for the night.

I didn't know what to think. I knew they were both

very cold the night before and didn't sleep well, but we were on a wilderness trip in Utah. Being uncomfortable at times was expected and is actually one of the reasons I enjoy camping.

We had planned to car camp that night; we had all our gear, food, and other supplies to make it an enjoyable night; and besides the slight chance of rain, the weather looked great - all making for a pretty comfortable camping experience. I couldn't understand why they didn't want to camp while on a wilderness trip in Utah. I was outnumbered and didn't have much of a choice but to ride back to town and stay in a hotel that night.

The trip was complete a few days later. I had mixed emotions about the trip. We completed a great backpacking trek, hiked many amazing trails, and saw what it was like to be on Mars. But we also did a lot of touristy things and stayed in a lot of hotels; this was not the true extended wilderness experience I was hoping for.

Despite the lack of prolonged solitude on the trip, I felt great about my outdoor skills and the decisions we made based on prior experiences. With the exception of choosing to complete a strenuous hike the day before backpacking, and the lack of physical endurance preparation, I was delighted by our overall wilderness aptitude.

Most impressive was Chris's heightened skills. He was very prepared for each hike and backpacking trek, had actionable knowledge of all his gear, packed the correct gear, and wore ideal clothing. Seeing how well we hiked together, and feeling confident in our abilities and wilderness aptitude, I was bound and determined to push all of our skills to the limit on the next trip.

8 - THE SUBWAY

Planning for our June 2017 trip began in July 2016, almost a full year in advance. Having visited many of the same locations two years in a row, I was seeking a destination that would be new for all of us; preferably an area with many backpacking trails, rugged terrain, and excellent views.

Chris and Josh agreed to attempt my bucket list hike in Zion National Park called The Subway. The hike would be technical with a lot of canyoneering involved, including cold water swims, rappelling, and difficult route finding. I had limited rappelling experience with the fire service, though Josh and Chris had none, so I was a little surprised when they agreed to the trek.

The permit for The Subway is one of the most highly sought after permits throughout the National Park system and is awarded via a random lottery. Only fifty hikers - made up of no more than twenty groups - are issued permits per day. Being peak season and on the weekend, there were over a thousand people applying for the same day as us; so we crossed our fingers and hoped our group of three would be drawn in the lottery.

In early April, a few weeks after applying for the lottery, we were notified that our application was selected for The Subway. Overjoyed with excitement, we began building our entire trip itinerary around the hike.

I spent days researching and preparing for our canyoneering trek in The Subway. There were many pieces of information that would help us prepare as best as possible in regard to equipment, clothing/shoes, self-rescue options, and trailhead access logistics. Using the power of the internet, I downloaded KML files (a series of GPS coordinates combined in a single file) to overlay on Google Earth, read as many trail descriptions and trip reports as I could, searched canyoneering forums online, and watched videos on YouTube of others completing the hike.

My first task was to determine what specialized equipment was required. Trail descriptions indicated a few rappels on the hike, but the height of these rappels varied across descriptions. An unknown was if rappelling anchors would be present, if we would need quicklinks and webbing, or would need to build our own anchors.

Compiling my research, I was comfortable planning for three rappels, with the highest being no more than thirty feet; and was also comfortable in planning for all of the rappels to have bolts and anchors already built and ready to use.

None of us owned any rappelling equipment, and knowing Chris and Josh had zero rappelling experience, I took on the task of shopping for all of us. I decided on thirty meters of rope, which would be enough rope for the highest rappel plus an excess of ten meters in case we ran into an unexpected situation - such as needing to use a natural anchor in the event of a broken anchor or bolt. Again, with Josh and Chris's inexperience, I went with a 11mm static rope, as the thickness would make it difficult to descend quickly or out of control.

In addition to rope, the rappelling required each of us to have at least one carabiner, harness, and ATC belay device. Ordering all Black Diamond equipment for myself, I tested it out, and then instructed Josh and Chris to purchase the exact same items.

The next task was to determine the best clothing and shoes to wear, and which packs to bring. The first few miles and last few miles of the hike appeared open and exposed to the sun, and since we were going in June, we had to assume the weather would be hot.

The middle section of the trail would be inside a slot canyon, with little to no sunlight. This slot canyon would require multiple swims in water that was expected to be very cold, likely in the mid-forties. Many online articles recommended wearing a wetsuit but doing so would require carrying the wetsuit over many miles of trail where it wasn't needed; or worse, wearing it while hiking in the hot sun.

I packed a polyester shirt and shorts to wear on the hike as my primary outfit and packed a long sleeve cold weather shirt and a beanie as emergency gear - just in case I became too cold after one of the swims. I contemplated bringing two pairs of shoes - a pair of hiking shoes for the dry sections and switching to a pair of Merrel water shoes and neoprene socks for the water sections. Ultimately, I decided on wearing just one pair out of concern for pack space and weight.

Since we would be swimming, I purchased a new twenty-four Liter Osprey waterproof pack. When it arrived, I tested it with everything I foresaw carrying. I placed my rope and other rappelling gear in it, along with water, food, extra clothes, first aid kit, knife, compass, and other emergency gear. It weighed about fifteen to twenty pounds, which was a little heavy, but I knew we would share on carrying the heavy and bulky rope. Even though my new pack was advertised as waterproof, I still planned to put essentials into a dry bag, such as my long sleeve shirt and beanie.

The park service always recommends bringing limited gear to stay overnight in the event of an emergency, as it may take a day or longer to get help. Calling for help deep inside the canyon would require someone to hike for many hours out to the main road; then depending on the weather situation, the time of day, and the severity of an injury, a rescue team may not come until the next day.

By packing my satellite distress beacon, we wouldn't need to find a road to call for help, but rather find an area with a clear view of the sky (a sometimes difficult task in the canyon environment). I also packed a space blanket, water purification tablets, lighter, headlamp, and extra food.

While watching a video on YouTube, there was an instance recorded where many hikers became trapped due to high water levels. One person was hiking alone and became trapped overnight next to rushing water in a small four by four-foot section of the canyon. Other hikers in the same video had to shelter in place for multiple days after climbing up the canyon wall to avoid the rapidly rising water levels. These hikers survived because they packed for the unexpected, including warm clothes, a space blanket, food, and a headlamp.

Since the trail was one-way, we needed to secure a shuttle to take us to the trailhead. I contacted the same company we used for The Narrows trip, the one that kindly refunded us due to the flash flood risks. The Zion Adventure Company had a shuttle advertised that would pick us up from the trail exit, Left Fork Trailhead, and take us to the starting point at the Wildcat Canyon Trailhead. The shuttle cost us $84, but there was no other way for us to complete the hike since we only had one car.

Lastly, I studied the map of the general area. I looked for areas of egress if we needed to get out quickly; I looked for trail intersections and side canyons that might be confusing. I really wanted to have the entire map memorized before we went on the trip, so if we lost our map, or if our phone with the downloaded map was damaged, I'd still know the route.

THE SUBWAY HIKE

Landing in Las Vegas on an early Saturday morning, we jumped in our rental car and drove out of town as quickly as possible. Our destination was Zion National Park. Having never been to the Kolob Canyons section of the park, and with a few hours to kill, we drove through the remote and uncrowded area of the park.

Backcountry permits are issued at both the main visitor center and the Kolob Canyons visitor center, so we went ahead and picked up our permit for the following day's hike in The Subway.

The rangers verified we had all the appropriate gear and maps, and provided us with a lot of useful information. We asked the rangers about the current conditions, specifically the water temperature and water level. The water level was reportedly at a normal level, but the water was colder than usual for that time of year.

It was suggested that a wetsuit would be appropriate, even though a few people had completed the hike over the past week without wearing one. Armed with valuable information, we thanked the rangers, took our permit, and headed towards our hotel in Springdale.

Just a few minutes' walk from the hotel, we made our way to the Zion Adventure Company to confirm our shuttle for the next day and to get another update on the trail conditions. One of the employees who completed the hike the previous weekend said they all wore wetsuits, but like the rangers had said, they noticed some other groups had not. Still unsure about whether a wetsuit was needed, we walked to another outfitter and had the same conversation with them, reaching the same conflicting conclusion.

I was torn between renting a wetsuit or not. If I rented one, I would have to carry the bulky suit in my pack during a large portion of the hike. If I didn't rent one, then I might get very cold; and with my slim stature, that happens very easily. Josh and Chris both decided not to rent a wetsuit, suggesting that with high temperatures forecasted in the mid-nineties, they couldn't imagine being cold.

Even though the high temperature for the day would be in the nineties, I knew we would be in the cold-water swimming sections of the slot canyon during the cool morning hours, when the temperature may still be in the sixties or seventies; and there would be very limited sunlight reaching the bottom of the canyon. With the mindset to better be safe than sorry, I decided to go ahead and rent a wetsuit for myself.

The evening before the big hike was very relaxed, consisting of eating burgers and fries at a bar and grill next to the hotel, and then preparing our packs for the next day. We double checked all our gear, filled up our water containers, and were in bed by 9:00 P.M.

***

Our alarms went off at a dark and early 5:00 A.M. Tired and not feeling well, I did not say more than ten words over our hotel buffet breakfast. Rather than being ill, my discomfort was attributed to a poor night's rest due to our unbearably hot hotel room and from heartburn/indigestion caused by the amount of fatty and greasy food we had for dinner.

When we walked outside to load up the car, we were shocked at how cold it was, especially since we were unable to get our hotel room to cool off. Even in June, nighttime in the desert can be cold, and without the sun's rays to warm us up, the fifty-degree air felt very cold. With sunlight slowly appearing to illuminate the sky, we drove twenty minutes to the Left Fork trailhead to meet our shuttle at 6:30 A.M.

Arriving at the trailhead fifteen minutes early, we lathered on sunscreen and took our packs out of the car. 6:30 A.M. came and went, and we became a little anxious having not seen the shuttle. We had hoped to get an early start to beat the heat and to finish at a decent hour, but it wasn't until 6:45 that the shuttle pulled into the parking lot.

Already onboard was a group of four hikers planning to backpack the West Rim trail over the next few days. As much as we would love to do the same, we felt a little bad for them, as the trail was very exposed to the sun and the forecast for the coming days had temperatures breaking one-hundred degrees.

Forced to wait an additional ten to fifteen minutes while the shuttle driver dropped the group off at another trailhead, we finally arrived at the Wildcat Canyon trailhead around 7:30 A.M.; about thirty minutes behind schedule.

The first 1.5 miles of hiking was very easy and very quick on the almost completely flat Wildcat Canyon trail. At the intersection of the Northgate Peaks trail, we were led out of the woods and onto an overlooking view of slickrock and canyons. Just a few hundred yards farther and we reached the turnoff for accessing The Subway. Stepping off the clearly marked trail and onto open slickrock, we headed east towards Russell Gulch.

It was here that the trail disappeared from the map and the route finding became a little challenging. We relied primarily on the cairns placed by other hikers to stay on track, but there were a few instances where the cairns either stopped or branched out in multiple directions.

The ability and luxury of pulling out my phone to look at the pre-downloaded map saved us a lot of time, as I could see our location relative to the overlaid trail. I pulled out the digital map as a result of drifting off course three times, but besides the aggravation and slight delay, it didn't affect our hike.

With the trailhead located at 7,000 feet and the Left Fork Canyon at 5,500 feet, we knew the hike across Russell Gulch would be downhill. Steep downhill hiking wasn't usually a concern, but the trail was comprised almost entirely of slickrock. After a couple miles of hiking on the steep slickrock, my feet began to hurt and had me rethinking the decision not to pack two pairs of shoes - one for the trail hiking and another for canyoneering. I was more than ready to reach the bottom of the canyon in hopes of a level, non-slickrock surface.

We had a tough time finding the descent into the confluence of Russell Gulch and the Left Fork, and we explored multiple paths along the cliff's edge. Once we found the correct route, we scrambled down an extremely steep path to the mouth of Russell Gulch and into the Left Fork of North Creek. From the trailhead to this point, we had descended 1,500 feet, which had taken a toll on our knees and feet.

***

Positioned at the start of the iconic canyoneering section of The Subway, we knew it was time to have fun. Ahead of us was a little over a mile of trail through the Left Fork of North Creek, located in a deep and narrow slot canyon. We knew the next hour or two would contain multiple rappels and cold-water swims. So, before continuing down the canyon, we sat down and ate some snacks, drank some water, I put on my wetsuit, and we all mentally prepared for the next section.

No sooner had we begun the canyon section of trail did we encounter our first obstacle - a large boulder blocking the entire canyon. Standing on top of the boulder, we were faced with a twenty-foot drop that would serve as our first rappel.

We stepped into our harnesses and secured our ATC belay devices, and I prepared the rope with the already in place anchor and quicklink. Giving both Josh and Chris a quick tutorial, I checked and double-checked their gear, and we rappelled with ease to the bottom.

The trail took us through many narrow slots that contained stretches of waist and chest deep water to wade through, as well as stretches clogged with logs and other storm debris.

It wasn't long before we faced a couple lengthy and very cold swims. One of these swims commenced from a three-foot drop-off - which inevitably meant our heads would be completely submerged when we jumped in the water - followed by a swim of about twenty yards. This also happened to be the coldest water yet, and afterwards we were all very cold - even me in my wetsuit.

With perfect timing, the canyon walls separated to about fifty yards wide, and we were provided a sandbar exposed to the sun. We stood still in the bright sun for about five to ten minutes in an attempt to warm up. With the low humidity and the direct sun, Chris and Josh dried out quickly, but I remained wet due to the wetsuit I was wearing.

Even with the sun bearing down, I was still freezing cold. We pushed on down the canyon in hopes of generating body heat, but after a few minutes of hiking, Josh said my face was turning blue. I removed the wetsuit in an attempt to dry off and warm up. It only took a few minutes to dry off, but unlike Josh and Chris, I was still chilled to the bone. With Josh worried about me, I told him I was fine and to keep hiking.

I suddenly heard Josh let out a yell in front of me. When I looked up, he was holding his foot off the ground, and he displayed a look of pain and discomfort in his face. I asked if he hit a rock with his leg or foot, hoping he had just a minor injury. But he quickly said "no" and indicated it was his ankle, putting my mind into gear about how we'd get him out of the canyon if his ankle was broken.

I told him to sit down, but he refused and said he was fine; it was obvious he was in pain. We all knew our location was the worst possible place on the hike to become immobilized; we could not go back the way we came, and we still had another rappelling and swimming section ahead of us. If he could not walk it off and keep moving under his own power, it may result in us waiting until the next day for help. This was the exact situation I was afraid of and had tried to prepare for.

The next few minutes were tense. Chris and I didn't say much, but we were already going through options and plans in our head. Should one of us go ahead alone? Should we wait and hope for another group to pass by? Should we activate the distress beacon to get help?

We never had to make the decision though, as after a few minutes of Josh gingerly walking around, he said he was good to go. I suggested we take it easy and not rush anything, as we had all day to get back to the car.

Pushing onward, the next swim was the coldest, and located in a long, shaded section of trail. Climbing out of the water following the twenty-yard swim, we were freezing cold in the now seventy to eighty-degree air, and we walked briskly in search of a sliver of sunlight.

Many minutes later, we found a beautiful opening right before the final rappel. We stopped, took off our shirts, and laid out on the rocks like reptiles soaking up the sun to raise our core body temperatures back to normal.

After a long rest stop, we walked over to the final rappel and took in the amazing scenery. The walls of the canyon appeared to be hand sculpted with perfect curves, textures, and colors. The amount of water flowing in the creek had increased dramatically, and a powerful waterfall poured thirty feet down into a narrow slot canyon, creating crystal clear pools of water. Finding the anchor a few yards past the waterfall, we rappelled down the final wall and directly into a frigid pool of water.

This section of trail contained the most beautiful natural formations I've ever seen. The section from shortly before our last rest stop all the way to our current location was the reason the trail was named The Subway.

The section started with a hike through a narrow tube, containing a perfectly formed cutout in the floor, exactly reminiscent of a subway tube. The narrow tube then opened up to a much larger formation with curved walls over forty feet tall; and then after the final rappel, continued on with numerous perfectly formed circular pools of water, mimicking the look of a hot tub. The many natural pools looked very inviting, but even with the air temperature quickly rising towards ninety degrees, our bodies were just too cold to voluntarily get in the water.

The last rappel also marked the point where hikers (also with a Subway permit) could hike to, following a non-technical trail from the Left Fork trailhead. The area was picturesque, and if you were to search online for The Subway, these are the images that usually come up. With the sun high in the sky creating the perfect lighting, I took photos from every angle possible, knowing it was probably the only chance I would ever have to be there.

I wished we could have stayed all day, but we still had another 3.5 miles of hiking through creeks, around boulders, and a 400-foot climb out of the canyon. So, we reluctantly continued down the trail, while the air temperature rose quickly; we were now fully exposed to the sun and would be for the remainder of the hike.

**

The trail followed the creek through a broad, open canyon. Crossing back and forth across the creek, the cold water now felt refreshing, and we walked directly in the creek whenever possible to keep cool.

Past the surreal scenery, we were ready to be done with the hike, but the trail just kept going and going. We hiked a fast pace and kept an eye out for the trail to depart the creek, which I had read was an easily missed trail junction.

Josh was hiking in front of me when out of nowhere, I

saw him collapse to the ground and let out a yell. I could tell that he rolled the same ankle that he did a few miles back, which was surprising as we were on flat, dirt terrain, rather than uneven or loose rock.

This time Josh wanted to sit down and was visibly in a lot more pain. After finding a log to sit on, he removed his shoe and we examined his ankle. An examination suggested that it was not broken, but with the amount of pain he was in, it was apparent he had sprained it.

Unsure if he'd be able to walk, we started thinking again of a plan to get help. If Josh couldn't walk out on his own, we were confident we could carry him to the start of the steep climb; but from there we didn't think it would be possible to continue without calling for help.

Without an Ace bandage to wrap the ankle - something that for now on we always pack with our emergency gear - the only thing we could do was find him a walking stick and give him some Motrin. After twenty minutes of resting, he attempted to weight bear his foot using the stick as an aid. He was in a good amount of pain but was able to make forward progress, although slowly.

Josh found a good rhythm, alternating between walking gently and hopping on one foot until we arrived at the climb out of the canyon. The extremely steep trail required a lot of flexing of the foot and caused Josh a lot of pain. Making matters worse, it was now mid-afternoon and the ninety-five-degree heat was amplified by the unobstructed sunshine. We rested every twenty feet or so and took our time on the climb, helping Josh where we could.

Eventually we reached the top and hiked the last half mile to the car. We were all very tired, sore, and Josh was in pain. All we wanted to do was drink water, eat some food, and rest. So, we headed back to town to drop off my wetsuit, and then headed to our destination for the evening - Kanab. We grabbed dinner at a local restaurant, iced Josh's ankle, and called it an early night.

I felt a huge sense of accomplishment after completing the hike. We all took a big step outside of our comfort zone by attempting such a technical and strenuous hike. I believe we were successful due to the extensive pre-planning that was taken before our trip, which I highly recommend for any trek into an area you have never explored before.

If Josh had indeed become immobilized due to his injury, I believe we would have comfortably been able to shelter for the night in the canyon and hope to find another group of hikers to go get help; and if we eventually saw none, I would have activated my distress beacon. The option I wanted to avoid at all costs was having someone go off alone or leaving Josh alone.

Me helping Chris prep for a rappel into The Subway

Josh, Chris, and I after the final rappel

Chris hiking through The Subway

9 - THIN AIR

BLUE LAKES

After our canyoneering trek into The Subway, we headed to Colorado for a few nights with the desire to hike to Blue Lakes, located between the towns of Telluride and Ouray. The environment was drastically different than the arid desert we had just come from. We now had lush forest, mountain rivers, and many 13,000 and 14,000-foot snow covered mountain peaks. The difference between this new landscape and the desert was like night and day.

We were pleasantly surprised when we arrived in Ouray. The mountain town was picturesque, nestled in a valley with towering peaks and waterfalls visible from the center of town. There were many shops and restaurants, and the town was bustling.

We were ready for a nap after indulging on a carbohydrate heavy meal for lunch. Driving a few miles down a gravel road just outside of town, we arrived at Thistledown Campground. To our delight, only two sites were occupied. We all slept relatively well that night, waking rested and ready to hike. Packing up the car as soon as we exited our tents, we quickly headed into Ouray for breakfast; and then to the Blue Lakes trailhead for what we hoped to be a moderately difficult and rewarding hike.

Located in the Mount Sneffels Wilderness Area, the trail was accessible by driving nine miles down a dirt road. We had been told the trailhead was usually crowded; many hikers use the trailhead for overnight backpacking trips as well as accessing the 14er Mount Sneffels. But to our luck, we were the only ones there at 8:30 A.M.

Our plan was to hike to the 11,700-foot Blue Lakes, located below Mount Sneffels, but still above tree line. The trail to Blue Lakes was only about four miles, but had 2,400 feet of elevation gain; so we knew the hike would be steep and tough. We threw on our day packs loaded with food and water, and we hit the trail with a fast and steady pace.

No sooner than we started the hike, Josh began to lag behind. While his ankle was still bothering him, it appeared the altitude was affecting him even worse; he was very winded, had a headache, and just didn't feel that great, all indications of altitude sickness. With nothing else planned that day except to hike the trail, we slowed our pace and kept going.

The trail ascended through a dense forest, offering occasional views of the towering peaks. After 1.5 miles, the trail entered the Mount Sneffels Wilderness Area, where patches of snow began to appear on the trail. Knowing we had another 1,000 feet of elevation to gain, I was anxious to see how much snow we'd encounter higher up. Soon after, the trail crossed a stream flowing quickly with snowmelt, and we reached a meadow situated not far below treeline.

We were at 10,400 feet. Josh's headache was throbbing, he was winded, and his stomach did not feel good; he was exhibiting many of the symptoms of altitude sickness.

There is no reliable way to know if someone is going to experience altitude sickness if they have never been to altitude before. This was the highest Josh had even been in his life, and while he was very well conditioned physically back in Georgia, his body could not make up for the oxygen difference. Physical fitness level at sea level is not predictive of the chance that an individual will develop altitude illness. Rather, genetic differences between individuals, as well as factors such as dehydration, acclimatization time, and speed of ascent influence each person's susceptibility to altitude sickness.

Essentially the body needs time to adjust many physiological processes, such as to increase diuresis short-term (days) and to produce more red blood cells (the cells that carry oxygen throughout the body) long-term (weeks). The factors that trigger these responses and the timing of each response vary by the individual.

Josh told Chris and me to proceed without him while he rested in the meadow, which we agreed to; we even recommended he slowly start descending back to the car. Since he would be alone, I left him with our emergency gear, including our first aid kit and a whistle.

Chris and I continued up the trail. The trail began to switchback through the forest and over open rocky areas. Chris and I had plenty of energy and were determined to reach the lake, but the snow had now completely covered the trail. The spring snowpack created conditions which we were not prepared for; we were hiking mostly on ice.

Even with slow and methodical steps, we were slipping and sliding all over the trail, and needed to hold onto tree branches in many spots. After thirty minutes of slow going and falling on our butts' numerous times, we threw in the towel and turned around. The trail was just too slippery for our shoes.

Rendezvousing with Josh at the meadow, he was full of energy and felt much better (though he still had a headache) after having an hour to rest and catch his breath. Heading back down the trail, we crossed the creek and had a very easy descent off the mountain.

Hikers coming up the trail began to pass us, many of whom asked about the conditions up top. We told them about the snow fields ahead, and while some were ill-prepared like us, others were expecting it and mentioned they had traction with them. This was the first time any of us had heard the term 'traction'.

Asking about what they meant by 'traction', they gave us a funny look and said 'microspikes' (microspikes are like small chains that are placed on your shoes to provide balance and stability while walking on snow and ice). If we had some with us, we would have easily made it to the top of the trail. I couldn't believe I wasn't familiar with these microspikes, or traction.

ASPEN/SNOWMASS

The following year we departed on a trip to Colorado and Utah. Now knowing about Josh's difficulties with high altitude, we primarily focused our trip to be in Moab, UT and Boulder, CO. After three days in Moab, we made our way to Boulder via an overnight stay in Glenwood Springs. However, taking note of high rain and storm chances near Boulder over the next few days, we decided to re-route our trip to the nearby Aspen and Snowmass area.

Josh knew we would encounter higher elevations by changing our trip itinerary, but he agreed the nice sunny weather at high altitude was better than the stormy weather in Boulder. With additional time to explore the surrounding area, we did a quick hike to Hanging Lake in hopes of helping Josh acclimate before heading to Snowmass Village.

Finishing the hike in about two hours, we then headed over to Snowmass Village and checked into our condo. The condo was only a five-minute walk from a variety of shops and restaurants and had a back deck with a great view of the mountains. The altitude here was 8,700 feet, making the June air crisp and cool, and added a little difficulty in breathing.

While carrying our luggage up a flight of stairs to access the condo, Josh became winded extremely fast. He was out of breath every time we walked up the stairs. At 8,700 feet, the level of oxygen in each breath was only about 15%, compared to about 21% back home in Georgia; which is why altitude sickness begins to occur in some individuals at 8,000 feet. I told him to just take it easy, drink plenty of water, and to avoid alcohol, and that by the next morning he would probably be acclimated to the altitude since we'd already been above 5,000 feet for four days.

A few hours later, after eating dinner and walking around the village, Josh was not feeling well. He had to catch his breath every time he moved, had a headache, and did not have much energy. He felt just like he did while trying to hike to Blue Lakes the year before; he was definitely feeling the effects of the altitude.

We decided to head into Aspen for a little while, which was about 700 feet lower than the condo. When we arrived in Aspen he felt a little better, but he went ahead and purchased a couple of containers of oxygen. The brand Boost sells small bottles of oxygen primarily marketed to hikers and skiers that come from sea level to Colorado for a quick vacation. Josh bought two large bottles which contained about 200 breaths each. We then headed back to the condo and watched Josh take hits off his oxygen bottles the rest of the night.

I researched hikes in the area that evening, specifically looking for a hike that was no higher than 8,000 feet and would not require a lot of climbing. Unfortunately, I could not find anything that looked intriguing under that elevation.

So I suggested we go to Maroon Lake since it was accessible by vehicle, figuring Josh would be okay riding there and hanging out by the 9,600-foot lake while Chris and I hiked farther up the trail to Crater Lake.

***

Josh was still not feeling well in the morning, so he offered to hang out alone in Aspen for the day while Chris and I went hiking. We drove Josh and his oxygen bottles into town and dropped him off on a corner.

It was already past 8:00 A.M., which meant we had to ride a shuttle to the trailhead. Being the summer season, the area was only open to shuttle buses between 8:00 A.M. – 5:00 P.M. due to the overwhelming popularity of the area. We purchased our tickets for the shuttle, and then boarded the bus for a twenty-minute ride to the trail. We texted Josh and let him know we were heading up to the trailhead, but then as soon as the shuttle departed, we lost cell phone service.

The shuttle dropped us off only a few hundred yards from Maroon Lake. We were immediately treated to a view of the lake and of the 14,163-foot Maroon Peak that served as a backdrop. We took some pictures and then began hiking the Crater Lake trail. The trail was uphill the entire two miles to the lake, but it wasn't very steep, climbing only 500 feet.

At Crater Lake, the view was remarkable. We found a spot on the edge of the crystal-clear lake to rest and enjoy the view; surrounded by steep mountain peaks including the Maroon Bells towering another 4,000 feet above the lake.

I took notice of many backcountry campsites around the lake, and Chris and I agreed we should come back in the future to backpack and camp. It would make for an excellent base camp during an attempt to summit Maroon Peak, something I have wanted to do since summiting the nearby Castle Peak many years earlier.

The day was absolutely perfect, with cool temperatures and blue skies. We spent over an hour lounging around and exploring the banks of Crater Lake. If Josh had been with us, I am sure we would have spent many hours hanging out around the area and possibly hiked farther; but since we had no cell service, we could not check on Josh to make sure he was doing okay. So, we hiked back to the trailhead and boarded the next shuttle bus back to town.

Picking up Josh in town, he reported that he was feeling much better as a result of the lower altitude and constant hits off his oxygen bottle. He said he took hits of oxygen all day, which felt great physically, but took a bite out of his ego, as everyone in town was staring and giving him weird looks.

Josh was envious when he saw the photos of our Maroon Lake and Crater Lake hike. He mentioned over dinner that he wanted to visit the lake but didn't want to ride on the shuttle. This left us with two options: arrive before 8:00 A.M. the next morning or drive up after dinner.

Wanting to sleep in the next morning, we got in the car after dinner and drove for thirty minutes to the parking area. Since it was after 5:00 P.M., we were able to drive the entire way. We walked around Maroon Lake under the moonlight, which was bright enough to light up all the surrounding peaks and give us a completely different perspective of the area.

Armed with his oxygen bottle, Josh felt fine walking around the lake. The rest of the trip, which was spent at less than 9,000 feet, Josh had no issues either. I doubt it was a result of the additional oxygen from his bottles but rather from his body having a few days to acclimate. Though he believes it was from the oxygen and says he will always purchase the bottles anytime he plans to be above 8,000 feet in the future.

10 – WILDERNESS CULTURE

STEWARDSHIP

Many of my trips have shined light on the disappointing fact that some people have zero or little respect for the land, wildlife, ancient artifacts, or fellow outdoor enthusiasts. Not only can poor stewardship lead to the closure of areas to everyone but it can also lead to permanent damage to the environment and historical landmarks.

While on a trip to Moab with Chris and Josh, we had an extra day to explore some of the more popular and easy hikes in Canyonlands National Park. While not necessarily a popular hike, Josh had read about an unmarked trail that would lead to an archaeological site called the False Kiva. When we arrived at the park, he did not quite remember where the trailhead was located, and without cell phone service, we were unable to search for the location. We stopped at a couple of pull-offs and followed some unmarked paths towards the canyon rim; but after doing this twice, and hiking for about three miles, we gave up.

This critical mistake of not researching the hike before we left may have cost us our only opportunity to ever visit the False Kiva, as two months later, the National Park Service permanently closed the site due to bouts of vandalism. Even a discreet location inside of a national park, with an unmarked trail that we were unable to find, was susceptible to vandalism.

This makes me wonder why the park service does not make the False Kiva an official trail in which hundreds of people would hike daily, as having more people around should discourage vandals and limit the opportunity for someone to get away with vandalism unnoticed. For example, we had never completed one of the most iconic hikes in Canyonlands, Mesa Arch. After our unsuccessful visit to False Kiva, we headed to the Mesa Arch trailhead despite the large crowds that were present. Mesa Arch is one of the most photographed locations in the park, both due to its beauty and easy 0.6-mile round trip hike from the parking lot.

We battled at least a hundred other hikers for a good view of the arch and almost became overwhelmed with the amount of people. But since there were so many people around, the opportunity for vandals to vandalize the site was eliminated. There were no signs of vandalism or damage to the formation, even with upwards of a thousand people a day visiting. We did notice a couple of people attempting to climb on top of the arch, but others immediately called out their behavior and asked them to stop.

Recently, I have noticed non-profit organizations being proactive in promoting stewardship in popular locations. On the Appalachian Trail in Georgia, northbound thru-hikers generally start their hike in the month of April. A few of these hikers have very little backpacking and camping experience. In an effort to properly educate the hikers, many volunteers and paid workers from the Appalachian Trail Conservancy patrol the first hundred miles in Georgia during the month of April. I encountered one such worker while camping at the Gooch Mountain Shelter at the end of April 2021.

He had been staying in the shelter's campground for the entire month and would hike ten or more miles a day on the trail. He made sure to stop and talk with every backpacker that came through the shelter, offering advice, tips, and planning resources. In addition, he made sure everyone was knowledgeable of trail etiquette and the 'Leave No Trace' principles in an effort to protect and preserve the trail and surrounding ecosystem. While it felt a little intruding to have someone observing our behavior, feeling like we were going to get into trouble for doing something he considered unacceptable, we had no issues. I think the program is great for educating and checking on new AT thru-hikers, and I hope the organization can increase the amount of volunteers or workers so more of the at-risk sections of the AT, such as on Max Patch Mountain, are protected.

Leading by example is the best method to teach others the common respect that should be given while in the wilderness. And being proactive is also a great way to lead by example, such as picking up another person's trash or calling others out for their inappropriate actions.

Simple concepts that may sound like common knowledge to many who read this book, such as the 'Leave No Trace' principles, are sometimes the most ignored by outdoor enthusiasts. While campers and backpackers will generally pack out their trash, a lot of times they will simply throw their leftover food out into the woods, or not disperse leftover firewood or extinguished charcoals back into the forest. 'Leave No Trace' means just that: if someone else comes to the same location as you a few hours after you left, there should be no signs of your presence left behind.

LOCAL KNOWLEDGE

A quick search on the internet or on social media will provide most of the top attractions, trails, and viewpoints for almost any location in the U.S. Searching for trails to hike or natural wonders to visit within Arches National Park will result in many wondrous results. Amazing pictures of arches and detailed trail descriptions are readily available, but few of the results will provide the great insider tips that can make a trip even more enjoyable.

On our second trip to Moab, we had planned a small portion of our trip around visiting and camping in Arches National Park. Having seen the breadth of things to do and arches to see, I felt it was best to obtain some insider information from the locals. Therefore, our first stop in Arches was the visitor center. The Arches Visitor Center was very large and informative. I found one of the rangers while in the visitor center and asked a few detailed questions, such as the best time of day to attempt certain hikes and inquired about how to make the most of our limited time in the park.

Talking with the rangers is always a good idea, since they are very knowledgeable on trails and areas not found in guidebooks or on a map. Many of the arches in the park are best viewed during sunrise or sunset, and the rangers know the best vantage points for each arch during different times of the day and can tell you about the least crowded times to visit each arch.

With the current weather situation, the time of day, the desired level of difficulty we were seeking, and the proximity to the campground we were staying in, the ranger recommended we explore the trails starting at the Devil's Garden Trailhead. We decided to hike to the Double O Arch while also checking out Landscape Arch, Navajo Arch, and Partition Arch. The enormous arches and rock formations were breathtaking and well worth the hike.

Just like speaking to rangers or park officials when visiting a state or national park, speaking with locals in the small towns can reveal many of the hidden gems to visit. While on a trip to Glenwood Springs, Colorado, we had seen a lot of Doc Holliday references while walking around the town, including a bar named Doc Holliday's Saloon. One evening after dinner we were sitting at the bar and asked the bartender why there were so many Doc Holliday references in town. She said that Holliday came to Glenwood Springs in hopes the natural hot springs would remedy his tuberculosis, but he ended up dying as a result of the disease while in his Glenwood Springs hotel.

The bartender shared with us that Doc Holliday's grave was located on the edge of town, up a short 0.7-mile round trip trail. She said people hike it all the time, even at night. It was already dark and we had nothing else to do, so after finishing our drinks, we retrieved our headlamps and walked through town in search of the trail. Finding the trailhead in the middle of a residential section of town, we hiked up the mountain to the graveyard and found the grave marker after a quick search. As an added bonus, the trail was located on the side of a mountain overlooking the town, giving us a great nighttime view of the area.

Another example where we sought information from locals comes from a trip where we visited the town of Telluride, Colorado. We planned to stay in the area for three nights but only booked two nights in a hotel. Rather than searching online for camping options, we waited until we arrived in town to inquire from the locals about the best options.

With multiple outdoor shops in the downtown area, we visited a few to garner recommendations from the employees. A couple of U.S. Forest Service campgrounds were recommended near the town of Ouray (about an hour away), so we planned to check them out the following day even though it was a longer drive than we desired. If the employees had not recommended the campgrounds, we probably would not have committed to such a long drive just to see if the campground was a viable and desirable option.

Driving a few miles down a gravel road just outside of Ouray, we arrived at U.S Forest Service Thistledown Campground. To our delight, only two sites were occupied. We walked through a few campsites and quickly settled into one. The area surrounding the campground was very secluded. Our campsite was located next to a large whitewater creek, surrounded by mountain peaks and dense forest. The sound of whitewater from all the snow melt drowned out any unwelcome noise from other campers, and the thick, lush vegetation blocked the view of other campsites - it really felt like we were alone. I packed an ENO hammock for the trip, which I set up on the creek bank to enjoy some peace and quiet for the afternoon and evening in a secluded, scenic, and uncrowded campground.

OVERCROWDING

Josh and I have visited Max Patch Mountain a few times and have camped there twice. The bald mountain overlooking both North Carolina and Tennessee provides amazing sunrises and sunsets. The mountain is made up of a large grassy field with a surprising amount of level ground, and with easy accessibility from a Forest Service road and parking lot, camping on the mountain is very desired and convenient.

Unfortunately, there are no rules regarding how many people can camp in the area and no enforcement of any parking requirements alongside the gravel road. I have been to this location three times, and each time it has been more crowded than the last. The most recent time I had to wait in a line of traffic for almost an hour just to reach the parking lot, only to turn back in search of a place to pull off the road. Cars lined the road for at least a quarter mile.

The mountain's popularity is warranted, and it is great to see so many people hiking and exploring the outdoors. But the area can only sustain so much human impact. There are no restrooms, no bear-proof trash containers, and there are many unofficial trails winding all over the mountain. Visiting the mountain on the weekend is unpleasant. The area reeks of human waste, trash is visible in many areas, and don't even consider camping near the summit as parties and drones will keep you awake all night. Why has the Forest Service not done anything about this area, such as requiring a permit, limiting the parking, installing bathrooms, trashcans, limiting the camping areas, and enforcing the already existing laws? That is a question that has baffled me for years, as many other areas across the country have implemented sustainable land use rules.

In July 2021, the Forest Service acted to address the issues at Max Patch. Camping was banned completely on the mountain, hiking off the official trail was prohibited, any use of the area was banned one hour after sunset, groups were limited to 10 people, drone use was restricted, and fires were banned. While I support the majority of these new regulations, I disagree with the banning of camping in the area, which applies even for AT thru-hikers. Designated campsites could have been established to allow for people to still enjoy the beautiful area overnight.

A great example of recently enacted land use rules is the Blue Lakes trail just outside of Glenwood Springs, Colorado. Chris, Josh, and I completed the hike back in 2018. We departed Glenwood Springs early Tuesday morning and drove to the Hanging Lake trailhead. The trailhead was packed, which surprised us since it was a Tuesday. The hike to Hanging Lake was rated strenuous, but was only a short two-mile round-trip trail; so we figured we could hike it pretty quickly. The hike started off straight uphill, and then continued uphill over the entire trek to the lake. In just one mile, we climbed 1,200 feet in elevation, making us very winded by the time we reached the lake.

Walking around the lake was like walking through a postcard. The size of the lake was small, about fifty yards long and fifty yards wide, and I would have labeled it a pond rather than a lake. The water was crystal clear with a blue-green hue, and was sourced by a waterfall pouring over a twenty-foot-tall ledge in multiple locations. The waterfall itself, as well as the creek leading up to it, flowed directly through heavy foliage and over roots, rather than a typical waterfall coming out of a well-defined creek or river.

The phenomenon was created when the lakebed collapsed from the ground a very long time ago, which also created an interesting exit point for the lake; the water did not converge at any specific exit, but it flowed shallowly over the entire southern edge of the lake, again through a heavily foliaged area.

The trail continued above the lake another few hundred yards, terminating at Spouting Rock. At the end of the trail, a powerful waterfall poured directly out the side of a cliff. The water was not coming from the top of the cliff like a typical waterfall, but rather out of a hole about halfway up the wall; giving the appearance that the rock was spouting water, hence the name Spouting Rock.

With the lake being absolutely picturesque, there was no wonder why there were so many people around. The popularity of the hike was unreal. Even with the strenuous trek to reach the top, many people were attempting the hike. Hiking back to the car, we were never on a section of trail where we could not spot another hiker; and the closer we were to the bottom, the more crowded it became.

Due to the popularity and the obvious overuse of the land, the U.S. Forest Service made major changes to the Hanging Lake trail in 2019. The changes require that all hikers must secure a permit before hiking, and the permits are limited to a certain amount per day. In addition, hikers are no longer allowed to park at the trailhead during peak season but, must either take a shuttle or bike to the trailhead.

These changes not only reduce the human impact on the trail and lake, but also keep out many ill-prepared hikers. With the trailhead located directly off Interstate 70, a lot of drivers had previously made unplanned stops and hiked the trail unprepared. With a permit now required in advance, only those hikers who have planned to do the hike are allowed to do so.

It was apparent as to which hikers had planned for the hike, and which hikers had simply decided to take a detour off Interstate 70. A quick glance at 10-20% of the hikers near the trailhead told us they would not make it to the top. The lack of proper gear alone was worrisome with many of the groups we passed. There were solo hikers and couples who were carrying no water, or only one water bottle. Other hikers were wearing improper footwear like sandals or slip-ons, or were wearing blue jeans. Yes, the trail was only a mile long, but it was very steep and rocky.

Proper footwear, like hiking boots or trail runners, are essential to avoid injury; and wearing blue jeans while hiking is almost always unadvised, as they are stiff, reduce mobility, and are made of non-breathable cotton.

An alarming number of hikers did not carry a pack, meaning all they had was what they carried in their hands. This meant they probably had no first aid kit, no food or snacks, or no extra water. While no one goes on a hike with the intent to become injured, to slip or fall, to get stung or bitten, to fall into cold water, or to develop heat exhaustion, the one sure way to make sure that an injury or accident turns into something more serious is to not be prepared.

While the permit system may help prevent ill-prepared hikers from attempting the trail, I have heard folks argue that requiring permits, especially permits that are difficult to obtain, may increase the overall risk and accident rates on hikes. The reasoning is the permits are only good for a single day. This forces the permit holder to hike on a specific day, potentially on a day of bad weather, such as extreme heat, cold, rain, or snow.

Rather than forgo the entire hike due to bad weather, since a permit holder does not have the option to wait until the following day for safer conditions, people are lured into hiking during dangerous conditions. Some areas have explored issuing permits valid for a longer timeframe, such as two or three days, but due to logistical restraints, this is not an option for many backcountry areas.

With the rising popularity of all outdoor parks and trails due to the 2020 pandemic, just getting the opportunity to enjoy many state and national parks is limited and sometimes difficult. Pre-planning weeks or months in advance is now required to enjoy certain parks as reservations are now required just to park in some locations.

For example, Zion National Park implemented a reservation and ticket system during the COVID pandemic in order to utilize the park shuttle. This would not be an issue if private cars were allowed to drive the main road and park at the trailheads, but the shuttle is the only method to access many of the trailheads (unless you wish the bike or walk many miles alongside the side of the road in the high desert heat).

The shuttle reservation system disproportionally affects low income and other groups. The reservation system is open only two days a month and tickets quickly sell out, meaning people must have access to the internet at that exact time the reservation system comes online – too bad for those who are working jobs that do not allow internet use during the middle of the workday. In addition, the reservation ticket is not free, and visitors are required to show an ID that matches the ticket before boarding a shuttle.

The reasonings behind these rules at certain parks are understandable. If the rules were not in place, then hundreds or thousands of people would try to visit each day unsuccessfully, creating traffic hazards and a lot of bad tempers. However, the parks need to create systems that are fair to all, such as having better timed intervals of when reservations are released, not charging ticket fees in addition to the park entry fees, and eventually investing in better infrastructure to support more visitors (as determined by the resiliency of the land).

Zion eliminated the requirement for tickets and reservations in June 2021, about a year after it was implemented. Immediately afterwards, the lines to board shuttles and even to commence certain hikes were long. Many times, visitors are required to wait hours just to board a bus. Then when visitors reached certain trailheads, such as Angels Landing, they are required to wait again to start the hike as the park implemented limits on the amount of people allowed to hike at a certain time.

As I mentioned in the Prologue, everyone should have the opportunity to visit and experience public lands. To continue this opportunity, action is required on two fronts: users of the land must continue to respect and portray stewardship, and land managers (local, state, and federal governments) must re-evaluate land use policies and determine how to best serve and provide opportunities for the entire community to enjoy the land, as well as educate visitors on proper stewardship and practices. And lastly, both the users and the land managers must communicate with each other clearly and effectively. Federal land policy decisions are communicated to the public and generally allow for anyone to comment during an open comment period, which can be done through the regulations.gov website.

This may be the best way for everyone to ensure the most effective and appropriate management of our public lands for not only us today, but for future generations to come.

EPILOGUE

The most rugged, towering, and awe-inspiring mountains I've ever laid eyes on were in Canada's Banff National Park. I had the opportunity to visit the park, along with many other areas across North America, while traveling for work. Traveling alone on many of these trips and with limited personal time, I couldn't explore the wilderness as I desired.

I was alone when I visited Banff National Park in early spring. Snow covered the ground and light snow showers intermediately filled the air. Trailheads and parking areas were abundant, yet desolate. The solitude felt by simply getting out of my car was unreal.

I knew the area was grizzly bear country and I didn't have bear spray with me, so being alone and with limited knowledge of the particular environment, I chose to hike very little.

The primary hike I did was around Lake Louise. The trail followed the bank around the lake, and therefore I never lost sight of the parking area. I felt confident that I could continue up the trail and into the woods, but I knew it wasn't smart since I was alone, hadn't told anyone my itinerary, didn't have bear spray, and didn't have my pack with emergency gear. But, even with the limited time and hiking I did complete in Banff, I knew it was a destination I wished to revisit.

Traveling for work took me to many other locations that I now wish to revisit, and I have tried to convince friends to go with me. My work colleague Joseph and I hiked a few trails in Idaho and saw beautiful rivers and natural hot springs while on a work trip. Returning there in the future, I would attempt a multi-night canoe camping trip down one of the many rivers.

Joseph and I also hiked many trails in California, including around Lake Tahoe, Malibu, and San Francisco. I was disappointed that my previously planned Yosemite trip with Josh and Chris had to be cancelled, so a future trip to California would probably include Yosemite and Lake Tahoe.

The most remote wilderness I've ever visited was Alaska. Renting a small camper, we drove everywhere from Denali National Park to the Kenai Peninsula. We stayed in completely deserted campgrounds, went whitewater rafting, hiked over glaciers, and saw an abundance of wildlife including grizzly and black bears, wolves, moose, and caribou. Even spending two weeks in the state, I left with a lot to still explore. I want to return to the state for at least a month-long trip to visit Kodiak Island, canoe camp on a river, backpack in Denali, and cruise through the Inside Passage.

I know I have limited myself to North America, but my desire to explore the wilderness across the globe is strong. In particular, the almost untouched and pristine environment of Patagonia remains at the top of my list. While the logistics would be difficult and probably require that I seek planning assistance from a guide, I believe my experiences have prepared me for attempting an extended backcountry trip of the region.

Also on my list, not too far behind Patagonia, is Iceland, New Zealand, and Switzerland. Switzerland in particular would make for a great blend of wilderness and civilization, which would be required if Josh and Chris were to join me. Since camping is only allowed in designated campsites throughout the Alps or above treeline, most backpackers use the first-class hut system. The huts are located throughout the country and are available for hikers to use as overnight stops on many treks. The huts are reservable, include food, and offer protection from the harsh mountain elements. Best of all, the huts eliminate the need to carry heavy and bulky camping gear and food.

When I wrote the first edition of this book, the largest hurdle to overcome in order to complete any of these bucket list trips was time. Finding a job that allows for enough time off to fully explore some of these areas is almost impossible. And then finding one or more experienced travel companions who have the time available and the desire to explore the same areas is difficult.

While writing the 2nd edition of this book, in the years 2020-2021, the largest hurdle to overcome is the global pandemic. While travelling has been difficult, I have been afforded more opportunities to explore areas close to home. But I am optimistic that many new adventures await, including many of my bucket list items, and that I can write another book in the next 5 years detailing my accounts of these adventures.

APPENDIX

NAVIGATING WITH GPS COORDINATES

There are many formats of GPS coordinates, but they all consist of two values. The first value references the latitude, or your relative location North to South. The second number references the longitude, or your relative location West to East.

The greater the latitude value, the further North you are, and the greater the longitude value, the further East you are.

One must be very aware of negative values. In North America, just like any location in the western hemisphere, longitude is a negative value (many applications no longer put the negative symbol in front, but rather put a W at the beginning or end of the coordinate, which is an incorrect format and can lead to confusion) with the exception being UTM coordinates which are a positive number in both the western and eastern hemispheres. Using decimal degree format as an example, -82.0105 is greater than -104.9903, meaning -82.0105 is further East.

If in the western hemisphere – as North America is – the closer the longitude value is to 0, then the further

East you are.

For example, using decimal degree format, if in North America and over an hour of hiking:
The latitude value goes from 31.555 to 31.655
The longitude value goes from -82.111 to -82.011
Then the hiking direction is Northeast.

If over an hour of hiking:
The latitude value remains at 31.555
The longitude value goes from -82.111 to -82.255
Then the hiking direction is due West (your hiking direction is taking you further away from longitude 0 – the prime meridian – and since you're in the western hemisphere, this means you are hiking West).

Using decimal degree format in North America without the negative symbol:
The latitude value remains at 31.555
The longitude value goes from 82.111W to 82.005W
Then the hiking direction is due East (your hiking direction is taking you closer to longitude 0 – the prime meridian – and since you're in the western hemisphere, this means you are hiking East).

Using UTM format, if in North America and over an hour of hiking:
The latitude value goes from 411556 to 411450
The longitude value goes from 3259818 to 3249818
Then the hiking direction is Southwest.

ESTIMATING DISTANCES

Determine an object within eyesight that you wish the know your distance from. Stretch your arm all the way out in front of you and hold up your thumb. Then close one eye and cover the object with your thumb.

Without moving your thumb, switch eyes so the eye that was closed is now open. The spot your thumb is now covering will be out to the side of the original object.

Using reasoning skills, estimate the distance between the original object and the new location that is covered by your thumb. It's best to think about something you're familiar with, such as the height of a nearby tree or length of a nearby boat.

Once you estimate the distance between the two points, multiply that distance by 10 and you will get your estimate distance from the object.

For example, if you wish to know the distance between you and a cell phone tower located across a lake, you'd first cover the tower with your thumb. Then, when you switch eyes, you notice your thumb is now covering a boulder off to the right or left. You need to estimate the distance between the tower and the boulder.

You spot a tree growing next to the tower that will assist in estimating the distance between the boulder and the tower. It appears you can fill the distance between the tower and the boulder using 4 of these trees laid out on their side.

Using the tower as a reference, you estimate the tree to be 75 feet tall. This means the estimated distance between the tower and the boulder is 300 feet (4 trees x 75 feet). Multiply 300 feet by 10 and you get 3,000 feet as the distance between you and the cell phone tower.

LEAVE NO TRACE SEVEN PRINCIPLES

The following 7 principles come from the Leave No Trace organization and can be found on lnt.org.

Principle 1: Plan Ahead and Prepare

Principle 2: Travel and Camp on Durable Surfaces

Principle 3: Dispose of Waste Properly

Principle 4: Leave What You Find

Principle 5: Minimize Campfire Impacts

Principle 6: Respect Wildlife

Principle 7: Be Considerate of Other Visitors

REFERENCES

© 1999 by the Leave No Trace Center for Outdoor Ethics: www.LNT.org.

Gonzales, Laurence. *Deep Survival*. New York: W.W. Norton Company, Inc., copyright (c) 2017, 2003

Trowell, C. T.. *Human History of the Okefenokee Swamp*. New Georgia Encyclopedia. 08 June 2017.

ABOUT THE AUTHOR

This is my first book ever written and probably won't be my last, so long as people read and enjoy it! I don't look to make writing my full-time profession, but rather I hope to entertain, educate, and share my experiences with others.

Follow Colby on Instagram @Colby.Farrow to view photos from many of the stories in this book.

Follow 'Colby Farrow' on YouTube to view video from The Subway.

Colby is a long-time enthusiast of the outdoors. Through a desire to share his stories with others, his first book ever written is The Part-Time Adventurer. He grew up and currently resides in Augusta, Georgia, yet feels most at home while traveling the country and exploring the wilderness.

Made in United States
North Haven, CT
08 September 2023

41325476R00118